CULTURAL DIVERSITY AND THE STRUCTURE AND PRACTICE OF ART EDUCATION

D1104475

by

June King McFee
Professor Emerita, University of Oregon

1998

About NAEA

Founded in 1947, the National Art Education Association is the largest professional art education association in the world. Membership includes elementary and secondary teachers, artists, administrators, museum educators, arts council staff, and university professors from throughout the United States and 66 foreign countries. NAEA's mission is to advance art education through professional development, service, advancement of knowledge, and leadership.

About the Noted Scholar Series

Cultural Diversity and the Structure and Practice of Art Education by June McFee is one book of many in NAEA's noted scholar series. The series was designed to recognize and honor art education scholars. The other titles in the noted scholar series are *Teaching Art and So On* by Edmund Burke Feldman; *Thinking in Art: A Philosophical Approach to Art Education* by Charles Dorn; *The World of Art Education* by Vincent Lanier; *Collaboration in Art Education* by Al Hurwitz; and *Revisitations: Ten Little Pieces on Art Education* by Harlan E. Hoffa.

©1998. The National Art Education Association, 1916 Association Drive, Reston, Virginia 20191-1590.

ISBN 0-937652-76-8

ACKNOWLEDGMENTS

I wish to express profound gratitude to: my husband and son, Malcolm and John, for their wisdom, tolerance, and sacrifices over many years; to my students who helped me focus the ideas, particularly Rogena Degge, who co-authored the last textbook, and to Jessie Lovano-Kerr, who worked as an assistant on the second edition of *Preparation for Art*; to my teachers, particularly George Spindler, from whom I learned cultural tolerance; and Claudio Alverez Tostado at Stanford who taught basic value relations between science and humanity; to Alexander Archipenko, the Ukrainian sculptor, who taught individuals to find their own way in art rather than follow his; and to Proceptus E. Costas at Whitman College, who taught languages as a source of social and ideational continuity; to all the members of NAEA who have helped build the institution and particularly the National Board who invited this material.

Finally, I am grateful to the University of Oregon that encouraged interdisciplinary programs among the arts, humanities, and sciences.

TABLE OF CONTENTS

INTRODUCTION

This monograph is in response to a National Art Education Association Board request to analyze my viewpoint on the nature of art education today. The intervening years and the immediate present are so full of dynamic action and reaction that a context for considering "What is today?" was difficult to bring into focus. Some history was needed.

This realization led me to develop a monograph of lectures and papers that addressed the changing nature of our society—its cultures and sub-cultures as they affect students, the functions of art in maintaining and supporting culture, and the content of art education theory and practice. The purpose was to provide more perspectives on past changes to help us grasp where we are today.

The papers focus on differences that culture makes on people's responses to and through art. Not included are materials I have written that used psychological analyses of individual differences in perception, cognition, creativity, and child development. Both approaches are needed in teaching. But in today's situation the most immediate and time-consuming concern of teachers are cultural influences.

Part One includes papers and addresses that analyze cultural diversity and its impact on art education. Each paper focuses on the changes in society at each point in time. It begins with my paper written for the 1965 Penn State Seminar, that lodestone in art education history where our interdisciplinary base was identified; psychology, anthropology, sociology, philosophy, art history, curriculum, and the practice and production of art in schools. At that time my focus was on the recognition of differences in opportunity to prepare to learn among American school children. My dissertation at Stanford (1957) and first book, *Preparation for Art* (1961), had investigated psychological and cultural differences among children.

Between 1965 and 1978, I was establishing and developing the Oregon doctoral program, writing the second edition of *Preparation for Art* (1970) and directing the Institute for Community Arts Studies, which built cultural ties between Art Education, Architecture, and Landscape Architecture with Oregon communities.

The second paper was for the International Society for Education in Art (INSEA) Conference in Adelaide, Australia in 1978, and was published in 1980. An extensive review of research in the social sciences was made to identify more of the functions of art in culture and education. The challenge to research and write this address was very important in my own development and much of the material is currently applicable.

The chapters that follow continue this inquiry in terms of the changing times. "Cross-Cultural Inquiry Into the Social Meaning of Art" was given to the joint Canadian Society for Education Through Art (CSEA) and the United States Society for Education Through Art (USSEA) in 1986. This was an opportunity to research beyond the INSEA conference, bring it up to date, and relate it to the changing populations. It reflected the escalating immigration of even more diverse peoples into both Canada and the United States. It also drew upon research in cross-cultural psychology, on cross-cultural training—the new field responding to the needs of international business—as well as new developments in anthropology.

In 1990 I was one of the members of the Fellows Symposium at the NAEA conference in Kansas City with Laura Chapman and Mary Lou Kuhn. My address is included here because it discusses culture change within the dominant culture of this country in relation to art, as well as in the other large cultural groups.

The Getty Center for Education in Arts Symposium, "DBAE and Cultural Diversity" (1992, Austin, Texas), included my paper, "Perspectives from the Social Sciences." It updates the development of the social science foundations of art education, the people, groups, and topics being developed at that time, on how art is valued, produced, and taught, as well as the ways it functions in peoples lives.

The most recent paper was developed for a conference on "International Trends in Multicultural and Cross-Cultural Visual Art Education" in Taipei, Taiwan (1995). The year before I had prepared materials for art teachers in Los Angeles County. Most of the world's cultures are represented there and their children are In those classrooms. The teachers were attempting to deal with the realities of all this variation in students art preferences, habits of perception, cognitive styles, values, attitudes and belief systems. It was from this basis that I prepared the paper for the conference in Taipei.

By contract, Taiwan teachers are working in a much less diverse setting—Mandarin Chinese language and culture is predominant. Occupation by 17th century Dutch and Spanish and briefly by the French in the 19th century was mainly absorbed. Japanese quite benign occupation from 1895 to 1945 contributed to the development of education and still has an effect.

Thousands of Chinese came when Chiang Kai-shek escaped from the communist occupation of mainland China in 1947 and established his government on Taiwan. Many of the art treasures were brought by him. This influx of people, the most recent government, and the ancient art reinforced the dominance of Chinese culture.

But this overall culture is changing rapidly. It has been very open to American and European ideas. Hundreds of its faculty in universities and teacher training institutions are trained in the West, in Japan, and Australia. It values education highly. Women are encouraged in education and in entering the professions and politics and all who are able are encouraged into higher education. Also, American and Japanese pop culture advertising and television are all seen as too pervasive.

Taiwan is now a leader in computer technology and a world player in electronics and other manufacture, as well as handcrafts and cottage industries. All this produces culture change and exposure to other cultures.

The focus of the conference on multicultural art was less on helping teachers work with diversity in their own country, but more on their ability to help their students grasp world cultures through art as their interface with the world increases and they face culture change from within and without.

A separate publication includes my research chapter on art and culture by anthropologists, cross-cultural psychologists, and other art educators (see Neperud, 1995, in Other Selected Bibliography).

Finally, in this section, I have included Chapter Two of the Second edition of *Preparation for Art* (1970). It still is a basic foundation for dealing with children from different cultures and relating to the arts that reflect and grow out of diverse human inventions of ways of life, values, social organizations, status and roles, belief systems and the arts they create to enhance, maintain, and change these systems.

Part Two includes three papers that address the structure of the profession of art education in a changing multicultural context.

The first is a paper delivered at a Supersession at the NAEA conference in Chicago in 1981. Here I laid out the foundations of art education that I saw as necessary for the field to meet the needs of teachers and students when the population was becoming so diverse. I put particular emphasis on the larger picture of the visual arts that is much more inclusive of the design influences on people's lives than traditional studio arts. Today I see this need as even more necessary because imagery is one of the most pervasive forces on people's lives, and design is its grammar.

The second paper is the 1990 Studies Award Lecture at the Kansas City NAEA convention. Here I identified the structure of the sometimes conflicting ideas that are present within the field and show how they can be mutually supportive rather than divisive. This covers the various ideas of "What is art?" the role of Western fine arts, crafts, folk arts, ethnic arts, and women's art in art education. The place of design in communication, environmental and architectural design, product design, graphics, costume, and the impact of the computer as an art tool is also analyzed.

We and our society are divisive about allowing for cultural diversity in education. The word *multicultural* has become an "ism" and unclean in some camps. The big question is considered, "how do we preserve our historically dominant cultural heritage and develop curriculum for our culturally diverse schools?" Also the dichotomies between theorists and practitioners, artists, and teachers are addressed.

The third paper is a report on the *Institute for Community Arts Studies* at Oregon, where bridges were built between communities and the University. It is included here because it was an example of cultural bridge building between academia and communities. Townspeople were helped to understand who and what they were because of the aesthetic and design decisions made in the past. It is also an example of ways graduate programs can be supported by field research which provides cross-cultural experience for both townspeople and art educators.

Part Three includes two papers written in 1975 and in 1981. The first was written to address the problems of women art educators in terms of sexual biases and professional opportunity, and was the first formal session of the NAEA Women's Caucus. The second paper, given at Miami University, focused on those experiences in both art and society that strongly influenced the concentration and scope of my work. Both of these papers give the reader insight into the factors that have given direction to all these writings.

Final Thoughts

To answer the question "Where are we today?" I would have to say that some questions raised in 1965 are still unanswered today. The problem is even more complex and building in much of the country. Resistance to change may also be greater than ever. I am encouraged that even with severe conflicts on national purpose, the reality of actual cultural diversity will force us to search for common ground. We must increase communications across perspectives and revitalize education as a central force in all of our complex society. Then art can be taught as a major communication system of education — a cohesive force for mutual understanding in a multicultural society.

1

SOCIETY, ART, AND EDUCATION

Penn State Seminar, 1965

The purpose of this paper is to stimulate further inquiry into the relationships between society, art, and education for possible directives for curriculum development in art. Identifying relationships among fields as complex as contemporary society, the broad aspects of the visual arts, and present day education is a nebulous undertaking. The materials that follow are based upon one individual's selection and analysis from the research and study that are available, and can only be presented to you within this qualifying framework.

Most of us would agree, I think, that this country is in a period of intense social change. Increased consciousness of minority groups and their emergence are challenging stereotypes and prejudice. Automation and population increase are affecting our concepts of leisure and of work. Social organization and human behavior are affected by the increase of megalopolis and changes in urban and rural environs. World problems, with the accelerating speed of communication and transportation, become community problems. Art educators' individual reactions to change probably run the gamut of those found among diverse groups in the larger society. We may be retreating from the changes by refusing to recognize them, or we may be trying to solve the conflicts they present with old solutions to old problems. Others of us may be overwhelmed into inaction by the complexities presented, or isolate ourselves by believing that our area of education or profession is not involved, that social problems belong to political scientists and sociologists but certainly not to individuals in the arts.

Our reaction depends in part on our concepts of the nature of art and its relationship to humanity. We cannot begin to explore the relationships between art and society without assessing our basic assumptions about art, for these assumptions condition our inquiry.

If we believe that art is to be produced and enjoyed only by an aesthetic and intellectual elite or subculture of our total society, then we might have reason for believing in social isolation of the arts. If, on the other hand, we consider art as a phenomenon of human behavior to be found wherever form, line, color are used to create symbols for communication and to qualitatively change the nature of experience, then art is related in some degree to all of society. If we accept this definition we, as art educators, become involved in problems of society and social change; we recognize art as one of the major communication systems of social interaction and of society in transition.

Definitions

The word *art* is often used to both denote and to qualify. We compare two objects by saying one is, but the other is not, *art*, when in actuality they may have many characteristics in common. Cultural anthropologists tend to identify most examples of visual symbolism and embellishment as art. This is a denoting, identifying function and does not necessarily make a value judgment about the quality of the art form. Much of commercial illustration is often derided as "non-art," yet form, line, color, and texture are used in some kind of composition or design to express ideas, conditions, or feelings. In our so-called "popular culture" we find myriad examples, where the elements and principles of art are used. The anthropologist would identify them as art. Further, the like-dislike behavior of a large majority of our students is learned within the context of the art in popular culture. As educators, we need a better structure of our terminology, so denoting and qualifying are not confused. We need other concepts and criteria for evaluating all the visual arts, fine, commercial, applied, to identify and evaluate their quality— integrity, impact, improvisation, organization or design quality and use of media. If we continue using art both to denote and to qualify we will deprive students of the aesthetic criteria they need to evaluate all phases of art.

As this thesis is developed it will become clearer, I hope, why the denotative concept of art is necessary if art education is to respond to the social demands of the day. Specifically, in contemporary society art is used in the full range from the sentimental to the profound, the superficial to the intrinsic, the commonplace to the unique, the repetitious to the divergent, the tawdry to the refined. Examples from each stage of these continua can be found in all of the major visual communication systems:

2

- those traditionally called the fine arts,
- in all product design including the handcrafted to the mass produced,
- in all advertising, display, and packaging,
- in architecture, city planning, and urban renewal,
- in television, publications, and moving pictures,
- in interiors and costume design.

Further, art exists in the present conditions of our cities and towns, representing many periods and copies of periods, in assorted states of preservation or decay. The whole broad face of America expresses values and attitudes through art forms and their condition. The art quality ranges from the sublime to the odious, and *students must have qualifying concepts to evaluate the whole range* if they are to make aesthetic discriminations as citizens in a democracy.

The Functions of Art

Art has varying functions in the lives of mankind which need to be considered as we develop curricula in art for students from various subcultures as they in turn are affected by social change. Some degree and combination of these functions of art are found in all cultures past and present.[1] Art is used to maintain the values, attitudes, and sense of reality from one generation to another. It is used to give character, identity and status to groups of people, individuals, institutions through mutually understood symbols—the styles of architecture and costume. Almost all religions use art forms to create their affective environment and stimulate the essence of worship. Political systems use non-verbal symbols to encourage recall of the values upheld. A symbol may have many meanings depending upon its variation. People with different backgrounds bring somewhat different sets of concepts into play when seeing it. The cross, for example, has pre- and post-Christian meanings and many derivations—a Maltese cross, a Latin cross, and a burning cross stimulate recall of different concepts and emotions.

Some cultures use art for "group-self-reflection" as in social criticism and satire; for education to identify patterns of behavior, eras of history, significant ideas. Finally, art is used in more subtle, but often more immediate emerging expressions of the essence of being and direct interaction, using less literate symbols of form and composition.

3

Culture and Society

The concepts culture and society have, like most terms, evolved with usage. They are sometimes used differently in the different social disciplines. In this paper *society* is used to mean an organization of people whose interaction patterns cluster them as a group. The United States is a large society that, through a system of government and interaction, separates it from other national governments. *Culture* is used to identify the values, attitudes, and acceptable behavior of people from a common heritage. A classroom can be considered a society as it has a pattern of interrelations among its members. Within the classroom there may be many cultures represented, children who have backgrounds that have influenced the development of quite different values, belief systems, and concepts of acceptable behavior. Cultures vary with different socioeconomic classes, religions, ethnic backgrounds, urban or rural environment, and geographic area. Our overall American society may have a broad identifiable culture, but it has many subcultures, large and small sub-societies.

Social class is identified by studying the ways groups of people relate themselves to other people, to economic level, and in some degree to behavioral patterns. Class stratification in this country is a reality that is often ignored by our idealism. Though there is considerable overlapping, shifting in an open society, there are identifiable differences between groups. They tend to share that which is called American culture, but they have distinct subcultural characteristics. Each ethnic group within a socio-economic class tends to vary in cultural pattern. Though social classes have general likenesses throughout the country, there are also regional differences, and differences if the groups are living in rural or urban areas.

A new term used by the sociologist Milton M. Gordon is particularly useful.[2] It is *ethclass*. He finds it necessary in describing the ethnic groups within the different economic strata of society. As more and more members of minority groups move into the middle and upper middle class, ethnic identification alone becomes inadequate to describe them, for they identify increasingly with mores of their social status. As this takes place more cultural diversity will be found within economic groups.

Gordon finds two conflicting trends in America. One is a pressure for conformity, due to middle-class oriented education and the extent and intensity of mass communications.[3] The other trend is that subcultures of race, religion, national origin, and economic level are much stronger than has been assumed.[4] This in-group cohesion and persistence of cultural values and attitudes shows signs of increase. Most people's primary group interaction is

4

within their subculture, while their secondary group activities tend to be within the larger society. Gordon finds that most of the professional and business leadership of the country comes from the middle class core culture, and from those members of other groups who have learned this core culture.[5] Another interesting trend which he identifies is the development of an intellectual subculture which includes some members of the academic community, the arts, and some of the upper levels of journalism, law, and medicine. Within this group ethnic differences are maintained by some, but there are also those who leave their ethnic subculture to become mainly part of the intellectual community.[6]

To those trained in education with the melting pot as an ideal, this pluralistic-culture with multiple value systems may seem paradoxical. Even if we decide that the core culture or middle class culture should be the focus of public school education for all American youth, we need to re-evaluate our goals in terms of the ethnic and cultural diversity of society. As art educators our problem is complicated by the fact that the middle class generally has not embraced the arts as central to its culture. It still has the stigma of being for an economic and cultural elite, and done by somewhat marginal people. Another contradiction emerges with the recognition of social class as a social reality by an educational system devoted to the preservation of an open society. The concept of the open society itself appears to exist within a middle class framework; that is, open from the middle class standpoint, and the school an institution for helping everyone become middle class.

Major Areas Of Social Change In America Of The Sixties

Now that we have discussed briefly some of the concepts describing the structure of American society, we should look at some of the major changes that are taking place which influence and affect all the segments in varying degrees and suggest some possible implications for art education.

Emergence of Minority Groups

Probably the most obvious single force in American society is that of desegregation of public institutions and services for the American Negro. Public desegregation and serious questioning of the rights of the states to dictate interpersonal relations between races have brought the question of the rights of all minority groups to the fore. The provisions of the civil rights bill open the door to more opportunity for many others besides the Negro; this means far-reaching social change affecting most of the society.

A correlative of the civil rights of the Negro is his transition from a rural to an urban resident. In 1900, 90% of the Negroes lived in the South and in rural areas. In 1960, only five out of every nine remained in the South. In 1960, 73% of the Negroes were urban dwellers; outside of the South 90% of the Negro population was urban. Some of these people are definitely middle and upper middle class.[7] They have the same goals for themselves and their children that other middle class people have. They take excellent care of property, their children are very carefully trained. But there are many Negroes among the new urban-population who have little or no awareness of the complexities of urban life, little ability to interact effectively within it, nor the skills needed to improve their living situations. The absentee landlord who continues to allow decaying slums to exist does little to help these people learn to help themselves. The magnitude of the problem of decaying living conditions with respect to the *sense* of identity and self-respect in the personality development of children can only be guessed.

The dynamic effect of the civil rights movement on minority groups that range from those who still live in degrading situations, whether they be Negro, Mexican-American, American Indian, or white, to those who have achieved the education and work opportunities to live with some dignity, portends to be one of our most serious problems. Some of these people will profit from civil rights so much sooner and in so much greater degree that the discrepancy between different Negro classes could cause even more volatile conflicts. Giving civil rights without giving economic opportunity and meaningful education could compound the social problem. All three are imperatives.

Economic Deprivation

The second change in American society is our recognition of the economically and socially deprived—the estimated 20% of our population who have less than $3,000 a year income per family. A large majority of these people are the undereducated members of the minority groups. Their young people are entering the labor market during the period when the children born during the post World War II baby boom are also entering the labor market. At the same time, automation is decreasing at a compounding rate, the number of jobs that were most often done by the less educated people. These three factors—automation, increased population among those entering the labor market, which creates increased competition and the need for more education—decrease the chances of many economically deprived persons and those in the social minorities from ever emerging from this depressed state. A very real question for the educator is: "How effective are middle class oriented curricula in helping these children and youth deal with their immediate problems so they can work for the future?" Is education broadening the gap even with the limited education many of these students are receiving? Is this the reason that the drop-out rate among them is so great—the gap between their immediate needs, their view of society, and that of the schools too great? Are they overwhelmed that the society that demands that they go to school really has no place for them when they finish?

If the stability of ethnic identification and *ethclass* as identified by Gordon continues, and if little progress is made for the economically deprived in the next decades, then grouping and stratification in our society may be on the increase rather than the decrease. The openness of our society in terms of upward social mobility may be more limited, at least for those who are now in the deprived segment of society.

The group of citizens most involved in developing school policy—the local school boards—tends to represent the white middle class core. If the needs of the students in our multicultural society are to be met, this leadership should include representatives of these groups. In many parts of the country this would mean that more Spanish-speaking people, more Indians, and more Negroes should be active members of school boards. It rarely happens now, and when it does the individuals are those who are an elite of their group, or have moved out of their background culture.

Implications for Art Education

In thinking of the functions of art in culture, and the social trends among minority peoples, what directives can we gain for art education? The *first directive*, to be sure, is that we need to do a great deal of research of the field of art, of the social functions and behaviors involved, as a basis for evaluating what might be possible to help these people. A study of the function of art in societies other than our own should give us insight into the way art forms, no matter how humble, operate in people's lives *right now*. We may have to be willing to look at these art forms with a new sensitivity to see how they function to give a sense of continuity and belonging to a community. If their art forms are making this contribution, then our introduction of art to members of these groups should include their symbolism. If not, we are in some degree teaching their children to devalue their own background. But one cannot make stereotyped judgments about children's ties to their background without knowing their *ethclass* as well, and the degree that they already accept or reject their background culture.

The American Negro is unique in his cultural heritage. Unlike the American Indian or Mexican-American who has a long-standing art background that may have meaning and remnants of meaning, the Negro has only the art forms that he has created in his more immediate past. He carried music forms from Africa, but his visual art forms were cut off. It appears that today's educated Negro's interest in African art tends to be intellectual rather than a culturally transmitted art form, available to those who have an opportunity to learn.

To understand the function of art for all urban people we need to become familiar with the cultural complex of our cities to identify the varied *ethclasses* represented. We need to make extensive study of the differences in values and attitudes toward art held by these various groups. Our sampling needs to include those who are working toward middle class assimilation, those who are middle class but desire to maintain ethnic identification. We need to identify the widely different segments of lower class society, to see what art might mean to them. This does not mean necessarily seeing how they react to the fine arts *as we know them*, but rather finding out how they may or may not use art in its broadest sense, which of mass media art forms are getting through to them. Attitude analysis will tell us what we need to recognize in beginning to make art experience of value, to relate it to what already has meaning for them.

Second, we need to take a long look at what we are teaching them about art. Are we helping children of these various groups preserve and develop symbols that help them preserve their cultural continuity, to identify and communicate with others in their same culture? Are we able to help them retain and respect their own culture at the same time that we give them the choice of accepting and appreciating all the visual arts? If we accept the concept of the pluralistic society—that it produces a richer, more varied national culture—then our art programs need to be developed at both the diverse and the universal levels.

Third, if we accept the function of the schools as an instrument for providing social mobility, are we including in our curricula opportunities for students to learn the discriminations and aesthetic sensitivity needed by people who do not learn them in their home environment. If we accept the assumption that the school has the further function of improving the environment, improving the standards of the core culture as well, then skills in art criticism need to be developed in language understandable to all age levels, and to encompass the broad uses of art.

Fourth, we need to look at cultures far removed from our own to gain perspectives for looking with more discrimination at the functions of art in our culture.

Ronald and Catherine Berndt are two Australian anthropologists who have made a comparative study of the diverse culture patterns of the Australian minority—the aborigines. They stress the importance of recognizing that these are contemporary cultures that have developed in different patterns from the white Australian, but not necessarily "different in quality or degree."[8]

Art forms and motives vary in the different groups. They range from naturalism to highly conventionalized symbols that can be understood only by those who know the meanings. Within a cultural group distinguishing individual artistry is apparent, yet a group pervasive is clearly recognizable. As groups vary in their art forms, a commonalty of quality that distinguishes Australian aboriginal art persists.[9]

Each art form has some degree of meaning. Some serve as a partial check on forgetting of complex verbal literature that is handed down for many generations.[10] Others reinforce religious faith by giving the participants a means of expressing their own religious experience. Religious ideology may be represented by series of key symbols of their belief system.[11]

The aborigine today ranges from the full-blood living very much as their forefathers did, in a slowly changing culture. Others have only a few words and memories of their past culture with which to identify, but are separated from full participation in their new, learned culture by their physical appearance.

If these seemingly homogenous peoples have this much diversity, we should gain insights into the vast cultural variety and symbolic meanings that may be found in our own country. The American Indian, the Mexican-American, the Negro, the Oriental, the New England white Anglo-Saxon, the religious and/or cultural Jew, the Irish, the Italian, the Eastern, Northern, and Southern European, the Southern American, the Southwesterner, the peoples of the newly cosmopolitan Pacific Coast all represent multiple social classes, cultural, economic, and social subgroups; and men's culture, women's culture, teenage culture all see symbolic meaning in somewhat different and changing ways.

As we analyze each of the major social forces we find that they are interdependent and *interfluential.* The implications for art education that appear important for one often apply to the others. It is only for the sake of clarification that they are separated.

9

Population and Urban Increases

The third major change in American society is the increase of population, compounded in its impact by the increase in urbanization and shifts of people within cities. In 1963 it was estimated that in three years there would be 10,000,000 more people in this country—and we are well on our way. If current projections materialize, there will be 225,000,000 people in the United States in 1975—ten years from now. In 1963 there were 50% more teenagers age 16 than there were in 1962; now they are 18 years old.[12] Think what this means to population trends when these young people become parents, even if the present slow decrease in birth rate continues.

The size of cities during the ten year period from 1950 to 1960 has varied throughout the country, but the national average is very high. From an analysis of 216 metropolitan areas the national average is estimated at 26.6%.[13] This figure represents the global area of a central city with its suburbs, whether under one government or not. Such growth puts tremendous strains on city governments to uphold standards for the overall city when the demands for expansion are so immediate, the money to be made from mushrooming housing developments so lush, and the tendency to crowd low income groups into less and less space per individual in the decaying parts of the cities so prevalent. In all cases, increase in population puts a strain on all existing facilities—schools, hospitals, care for the aged, transportation, law enforcement, and recreational facilities.

All these pressures of immediate problems to be solved tend to direct less and less attention to the aesthetic quality of our cities. The value on expediency, getting things done as quickly as possible, that is so much a part of our expanding economy, allows little time for the solving of the practical problems of city growth in terms of the long range *visual effect* of the cities themselves.

These trends all point to the critical necessity of educating more people in the visual arts, so that this period of what may become the *greatest growth of cities* will not result in more and more ugly monotony as slums are renewed, in bland and impersonal areas that have little color or cultural meaning. When the problem of the increased numbers moving into cities is compounded by the percent of these people who are ill prepared for living in urban areas of complex and diverse cultures, we see how important art becomes as a means of developing a sense of community through variation in meaningful design and symbolic communication.

The complexities of city planning often leave the human dimension with much less attention than it deserves. Planning is often concerned with the acute problems that are easily measurable—traffic congestion, the need for better access to services and goods, housing in terms of statistical averages. Real estate boards and vested interest groups often live within their own economic and social group cultures and tend not to think in terms of the whole city and the diverse cultural groups within it. Though leading architects and urban designers are often social architects as well, many magnificent plans for urban renewal do not consider the cultural or the aesthetic needs of people. Even the aesthetic needs are often in terms of an educated elite, not the population who will use the housing.

I do not propose that our levels of taste would be reduced to some common denominator, but rather that designers and architects be aware of the cultural diversity and plan so that the life patterns of people are not needlessly destroyed, rather that they are maintained, enhanced, and developed. At the turn of the century the emergent new plans for developing our cities had the "*melting pot*" as a basic assumption. Plans for renewal after World War II were based on the assumption that population would stabilize, and were made for a much smaller population than was actually born or migrated into the cities.

Henry S. Churchill, the architect, in his well-titled book, *The City Is The People*, pleads with city planners to review the old plans of the last fifty years, to see how inadequate they have been in effectively dealing with the situation as it actually exists. He is among those architects who are concerned with the social and psychological life-space of the people who make up the city. He asks for preservation of areas of color and imagination, as well as opening space, for diversity rather than planning by averages which don't really fit any group's way of life.[14]

In part, a long-standing tradition needs to be broken. The architect has traditionally been a designer for the elite or large organizations which were responsible for other parts of society. Today this is exemplified by architects working for metropolitan districts, for large insurance companies that invest in what has been planned to be slum clearance. European city planning, because of the necessary rebuilding due to World War II, has included more effective housing for low income groups. In this country no one bombed out our slums, there is money to be made in perpetuating them, so our renewal trails far behind in terms of our capacity to produce.

Another American tradition—the rights of the individual—has been distorted into a callous disregard of society's natural and aesthetic resources. Our air and our countryside have been treated as *private* domain to serve the cause of monetary progress, irrespective of the visual consequences in the *public* domain. *To stress each citizen's responsibility, to evaluate the quality*

11

of his aesthetic contribution to the public view, in the face of the tradition of socially irresponsible individualism, may be crying in the dark. But the public reaction to air and stream pollution, the President's plea for a beautiful America, the progress made by responsible industries, may encourage public support for art education in helping students gain the capacity for critical aesthetic judgment as part of their civic responsibility.

Another shift that needs to be made in our thinking is the idea that something that is well-designed according to our tastes will have meaning to other people as well. We are extremely egocentric as a people, seeing the world only through our own eyes and through our own *ethclass* values. It seems to me that art educators must take responsibility for a much wider curriculum. Certainly, our long standing goal of helping individual children and youth acquire an open avenue of expression through art is as important as ever. As we have less geometric space in which to live, the development of self-direction and expression is important, but understanding design as communication, and its myriad application and use in creating rich and meaningful environments in our multifaceted and increasingly complex society is needed as well. We cannot allow people to grow up as visual and aesthetic illiterates and expect them to be aware of their aesthetic responsibilities as citizens.

Automation and the Increase of Leisure

Programmed production and the decreased work week, somewhat independently of each other, are influencing a fourth area of change in American society. Automation is increasingly accelerating the long range decrease of working time that has been going on during this century.

The Darnell Corporation survey of 342 United States and Canadian companies points out a recent and decided trend toward the reduced work week, particularly when vacation time is included in yearly work patterns. Prior to World War II only one worker in four got a paid week's vacation. Between the two decades of 1940 to 1960, the total working time for the average worker dropped the equivalent of four weeks. In the last five years, a great increase in vacation time has developed, with half the salaried workers getting a month's vacation sometime in their career. Paid holidays have increased in 25 years from an average of two to over seven. Now if a person works on a new job six months he gets a week's vacation, a year's work qualifies for two weeks, after three to five years the period is three weeks, and after ten years, a month. At present, one in four workers in this sample works between 32 and 40 hours a week.[15] The main trend indicates that there will be more people with leisure time than ever before in the history of mankind. Now the machine is freeing vast numbers for leisure that they have neither cultural pattern nor cultural training to use. Decrease in work creates both leisure and unemployment, but the unemployed have no leisure if it is defined as the time one has beyond gainful work.

One of the most crucial problems of automation is what it does to the new worker, the young man or woman with or without a high school education. Automation is cutting down most drastically in those kinds of unskilled jobs in which young people got the experience they needed to move up in the labor market. As the 1947 war baby population enters the labor market, this will probably increase the percentages of unemployed youth.[16] These same unemployed youth, if these conditions continue, will have fewer opportunities for a first job. It was reported in the winter of 1965 by the Population Reference Bureau that over 1/4 of the 1947 baby boom, now aged 17, are out of school and looking for work.[17]

The Negro and the under-educated are most affected. In 1962, 11% of the non-white members of the working force were not working, compared to only 4. 9% of the white members. It still remains twice as high. Among all groups, 2/3 of the unemployed had not finished high school. The overall percentage was 9% for those who had not finished 9th grade, 7% for those who had not finished high school, but only 2% for those with some college education.

One of the longstanding concepts that has underlain much of our past history has been that *those who work* have a *right to income*, and income is necessary to life. We have assumed that we could carry a certain number of people on relief. Now we are faced with a revolution in the nature of work in which the machine replaces people. We are faced with having to decide whether or not we will change our concepts of what work is, what would be repaid by society for service to it, or whether we shall consign more and more people to lives of inaction and poverty. In a succinct publication of the Center For the Study of Democratic Institutions, Gerald Piel and Ralph Helstein discuss the relation of work to income as follows:

> Helstein: I accept the fact that full employment at this juncture in
> time is a misleading goal if by full employment is meant the tra-
> ditional kind of jobs in the private market—a market that has
> failed in the last five years to produce the kind and number of
> jobs necessary. A revision of our concept of work is required.
> After all, work is only what society says it is. There is no reason

13

why we cannot start redefining our notions of what work is and in this way provide full employment...[18]

Piel: The underlying scandal of what we are talking about here is that the market economy offered and promoted kinds of work that were sanctioned by the values of the market and the profits system. The function we are talking about, the people-to-people function, is notably not conducted for profit or market-generated ... We are talking in terms of fundamental changes in our society that go beyond the emergency measure of providing an income for everybody, to building a society with an entirely different set of values about *what qualifies* as *socially useful work.*[19]

As we reflect on what these men have said, and think about the arts, we may gain some insight. The arts and the artist have long been outside the mainstream of American life. Though gaining in prominence, the stereotype of the artist is still not an ideal personality type to which young people may be motivated. As this change in the concept of work takes place, will we in the visual arts be ready to provide the impetus and education so that the arts can become central activities in socially useful work—improving our cities and our homes, and the quality of our experience, as well as contributing to the quality of production; *in creating new dimensions for communication which have symbolic and aesthetic meaning in our diversified society*? Can we help more people contribute to society through art, who are now denied admission to the market economy?

As concepts of work and play change, our evaluation of leisure will of necessity change. One possible explanation of the reticence found in American education against accepting education for leisure in the elementary and high schools has been our Puritanical tradition that non-work is somehow related to sin. Though the social structure of American life is changing, the concept of a college education as a doorway to the good life, which includes the right to leisure, has preserved the liberal arts in higher education. To educate for leisure below that level has somehow seemed unimportant because we have assumed that only the elite have the right to leisure. The further stereotype that the arts are the play of the leisure elite, and the artist a social deviant, because he participates little in the mainstream of economic gain, have contributed to the peripheral position of the arts in public school education.

As art educators we have felt the need, and in part rightly so, to defend the artistic dimension as vital to good economy, long range planning in cities, the development of significant communities, and a necessity for improved production. At the same time, the nation as a whole must recognize that increased population, automation, and the decreased work week mean that a majority rather than a minority of society will be in the leisure class. So we must educate the public to recognize that education in the visual arts is vital to the development of citizens in our society because it is one of the primary communication systems, and that it is also a means of individual and collective development during leisure.

Mass Media And Its Effects On Social Change

Mass media is a major factor to be considered in social change. It accentuates the differences between its general standard of mediocrity and commonalty and the diversity of cultures and economic levels. It purports, through advertising, to identify the so-called good life which anyone can achieve if [he or she is] just able to buy the right products. Paul Hoffman identifies rising expectations, as a result of increased communication and transportation, as one of the most crucial factors in international affairs. He writes: "... rising expectations" are "...one of the most powerful forces affecting the future of mankind." He cautions that one face of the movement is a desire for progress which we must help or we will have "...the other face turned upon us. This is the ugly face of violence and even chaos, born from hopeless frustration and despair..."[20]

At the same time that the open door to opportunity seems to be closing due to increased automation and population, these same people in *this* country are able to see at least a distorted picture of the affluent society. We need careful content analysis of the values being projected through mass media, as well as continued study of the diversity of values in American society, to be able to understand the conflicts, the anxieties and frustrations that television, for instance, may produce among children from deprived segments of society. There has been extensive concern over the violence on television, but little for this more subtle influence with its distorted picture of "the good life" in creating hostility and frustrations among the economically deprived.

In another report of the Center for the Study of Democratic Institutions on the nature of the American Character, Jack Gould, Television Critic of the *New York Times,* analyzes the power structure of American television, and the decision-making that goes into the selection of programs. He states: "...the real control rests with the sponsor. By the act of not purchasing certain kinds of programs the sponsor exercises a tremendous force on television programming. The sponsor's negative power is enormous ...he has a power of veto over what the public sees; he simply does not buy that program."[21] News and public affairs programming are the two areas where, as he says, "Sponsors, to their credit, have kept their hands off." It is in the area of creative writing for television that Gould finds the greatest disaster, both to the arts and to society. Nothing controversial that is to be found on the contemporary scene can be used. Only those writers survive who are well-trained "in the taboos of the business." Further, the uncreative, plot-repeating westerns, situational comedy, horror and gangster programs come when the greatest viewing takes place, from eight to eleven at night. Sunday mornings and late evenings provide the main alternatives. Any book shop, any news stand, any record store provides the consumer with a far greater choice. But for many the window on the good life, the advertising that accompanies their diversion, is not only a farce on life, but is also unattainable.[22]

The major question which the impact of television and mass media on society raises for us is whether we do, or can, give students the tools with which to evaluate the obvious and the subtle messages of this one-way communication system. *We have the obligation to try to offer students more alternatives*. This requires that we be aware of what they are receiving; that we analyze the art forms being used so that we may help them develop and use aesthetic criteria in their evaluations.

Anomy

The final social force is "anomy" in American society. Merton defines it as a "breakdown in the cultural structure, occurring particularly when there is an acute disjunction between the cultural norms and goals and the socially structured capacities of members of the group to act in accord with them," or to put it in other words, situations where the individual cannot relate himself to his perceptions of the norms of society, resulting, among other feelings, in a sense of isolation. What happens to individuals also appears to happen to groups of individuals.

Sociologists and social and personality psychologists disagree as to whether or not anomy is increasing. Durkheim and Merton deal with social conditions and their relationships to deviant behavior. Others, mainly psychologists, are concerned with the kinds of personalities which, in response to certain kinds of social situations, become more deviant in behavior. Those who study personality factors in anomy feel that one cannot evaluate the trend of the overall society as being more or less anomic unless one identifies the point of view of the observer.

McClosky and Schaar, in a review of the literature and their own study of national and Minnesota samples, report that anomy is found mostly among old people, widowed, divorced, and separated; under-educated, persons with low incomes or with low prestige positions; people moving downward socially; Negroes, foreign-born, and non-city dwellers and farmers.[23]

They feel that these people have less opportunity to interact and communicate within the dominant society, and thus have less opportunity to "see and understand how the society works and what its goals and values are."

Anomic feeling may come from the social situation for some people, from their own personalities in others, or can be a combination from both sources.

In a comprehensive series of tests, administered to random national and Minnesota samples, these researchers find the following trends. *Low anomy* correlated highly with high education, intellectuality, high tolerance for ambiguity and those who take social responsibility. *High anomy* was correlated most with low education and intellect, *intolerance* of the ambiguous, dependence on black and white answers, and low social responsibility. Using the totals for their figures on tolerance, I found the following percentages of persons high in anomy: 35% of the people in the national sample and 28% of those in the Minnesota sample were high in anomy.

Some percentages of these people were found in all economic and educational levels, though predominantly found among the under-educated, under-privileged, the rigid and anxious who have less opportunity for social interaction with the dominant society through "communication, interaction, and learning..."

Whether these figures represent an increase or not, they do represent a serious situation which should concern educators, for it apparently concerns one in three students. The big question for the art educator, it would seem, is: how can art experience and symbolic communication contribute to the sense of identity and social participation of these people? Many of them will be found among our new urbanites, certainly among the economically and socially deprived. This dimension of psycho-social behavior, like the "*eth-class*" becomes a confounding but useful tool if we are really concerned about developing art curricula that can have meaning to all American children and youth.

These are the *key issues* as I see them. What do they mean to us? Some investigators of American society feel that this is the era of greatest rapidity of change in human history. This means that we need greater flexibility in our use of categories, more awareness of the possible alternatives to our assumptions, than ever before. At this point, we may feel we have opened a Pandora's box by looking so briefly at complex social factors that are acting and reacting upon each other to change our way of life. A caution is needed here. Culture does persist, attitudes and values sometimes remain beyond their usefulness, but in our haste to meet the challenge of change, we may heedlessly throw out values that have continuing importance. For example, when some of us plead for the use of more intellect in art education to solve aesthetic problems in modern society, we should not negate the use of *intuition*, *improvisation*, or even *personality projection through art*. Because we believe that art has a place in the lives of all people does not deny the right, and society's need for, an *aesthetic-creative elite* to break the barriers of artistic discovery. The recognition and encouragement of the best in the fine arts does not necessarily have to negate, as non-art, the ethnic and popular arts that have meaning to large segments of society. *We need only to ask that the students develop evaluative criteria for responding to all the visual arts.*

Review And Implications For Art Education

In summary, the big forces in social change that have implications for art education are as follows:

First, we find that American culture, as studied by sociologists interested in social diversity, is much more complex than we may have imagined. Subcultures appear to maintain their characteristics even when they change socio-economic levels.

Second, minority groups are emerging into fuller citizenship roles through increased civil rights, but within these groups the opportunities to utilize these rights varies significantly.

Third, the plight of the economically and socially deprived is not helped by automation, population increase, and the decrease of jobs, even though civil rights may give them more right to opportunity.

Fourth, the increase in population that are centering in urban areas, the increase of megapolis, is bringing many people to cities who know little of the ways of city culture. Urban renewal without some education and continuity from past culture may create new problems of anomy, and new slums.

Fifth, automation is decreasing the number of jobs, particularly for the undereducated. The chances of entering the labor force are decreasing for the under-educated minority youth. Further, automation is decreasing the need for working hours. More people will have more time for leisure than they need to earn a living.

Sixth, mass media, at present, is making shallow use of the arts to present a picture of the good life which centers around the use of its products. The pressure to enter the so-called good life through acquisition of the proper products comes at the same time that automation and increased population, in combination, decrease the purchasing power of approximately one-fifth of our people. At the same time, there are combinations of factors; automation, increased population, that appear to be decreasing opportunity in our society, as society as a whole is beginning to be aware of its social responsibility to all members.

Seventh, anomy, social isolation, operates to compound the problems. Those who are most separated may be the most easily affected by society's lack of recognition of its diversity, and by decreased opportunity to operate in the dominant society.

Our question then becomes: what can we as art educators do to begin to deal with these problems as we try to cope with the education of all children and youth? What follows is only my own attempt to try to identify the kinds of behaviors requiring aesthetic judgments that appear to be needed by the members of our society, and then to postulate some directives for art education.

The first deals with rural people learning to live in crowded cities, and slum dwellers moving into urban renewal.

1. Preserving, through their own creation, the symbolism of their background culture if it has meaning for them.
2. Developing independent judgment in evaluating what is presented to them in the city.
3. Learning to take responsibility for their contribution to the public view.
4. Learning basic skills in production and maintenance of what they do possess.
5. Becoming aware of the differences between order and disorder, and the differences in impact these have upon themselves.
6. Learning ways to make order and variation through groupings of color, of forms, of line and textures, etc. with minimal materials.
7. Developing new avenues of socially useful work through art.

Teachers who attempt this will need to be prepared to understand cultural, economic, and personality differences among groups of children so that the initial comparisons are with things that have meaning to them. In some way the goals of the teacher will have to be related to the goals the students have for themselves—which in many cases will be the goals given them by mass media. By attempting to start where they are, with what is important to them, a beginning can be made. If art is not related to their own past experience, to their own goals, the beginning experiences upon which further learnings in art can be built will not take place. This is as true in teaching middle class children, where art is not respected in the home, as those whose folk art or lack of art has not prepared them for using art in their civic and social responsibilities.

A question I can see being raised by some of us is: "Lots of kids from most deprived backgrounds are very expressive once they get a chance to use some art material. Why all this emphasis on differences in background?" My answer to this is to agree in part. I've had the exciting experience of watching hostile, rejected students pour out their feelings with paint. I wouldn't discourage this kind of communication. But does this help these youngsters make aesthetic judgments to improve the quality of their experience? Does it help them preserve their own unique background and still help them contribute to the life of those around them? Does it help those who don't open up in this kind of experience, to find art operative and useful in their own lives? Will self-projection alone open up avenues for art in the new dimensions of what is to be called work, that some of our sociologists see as necessary in the immediate future?

Some of these behaviors we have discussed are needed by all children in this mobile society where people change their residence so often. The following are some aesthetically based behaviors I believe should be considered in all art education:

1. Helping students see the functions of art in culture as it transmits values and attitudes, and identifies cultural meanings.
2. Helping students respect and understand cultural pluralism in our society by becoming aware of the functions of art in our many subcultures.
3. Helping students recognize the importance of the aesthetic dimension in the economic and political decisions of civic affairs, in urban and rural renewal, conservation, city planning, and neighborhood development.
4. Helping students discriminate and evaluate the symbolic communication of mass media to preserve independent judgment.
5. Helping students understand the uses of intuition and creativity so that the arts can become avenues for self-directed use of leisure.
6. Helping students understand the multifaceted interaction of the elements of design so that they may develop a basis for aesthetic discrimination

7. Helping students to differentiate between social aesthetic responsibility and individual divergent creativity; to develop and preserve the uniqueness of the individual while increased population and decreased space require more cooperative planning and social responsibility.

8. Helping the artistically gifted to recognize their responsibilities to society as designers, artists, and architects.

To further develop these objectives, we in art education face several tasks. We need to know a great deal more about the functions of design, its structure, so that we can teach it to people of widely divergent backgrounds. We need to study the differences in values and attitudes about art and about the life of many more groups of people. Certainly this includes becoming aware of our own basic assumptions about art and its relation to life as we understand our own unique backgrounds. Finally, we need to do considerable classroom research in means and methods of making design meaningful and usable in all segments of American life.

We must become *increasingly* aware of the political, economic, cultural realities of our cities today as they affect the rapidly changing society, if we wish to make the aesthetic dimension felt. We need to teach art in general education so that all concerned with the city and its development—its managers, planners, economists, and its electorate—are keenly aware of the aesthetic impact of their decisions on the lives of people. Further, we must so understand the cultural diversity of students so that art will have meaning in the lives of more and more people, to preserve culture, to enhance their day-to-day living, and preserve their group uniqueness and their individual identity.

We in art education can probably contribute only a small part to the solution of our nation's monumental problems, but we cannot even begin unless we are more aware of the complexities and dynamics of change which we face. In teacher training, in curriculum development, in research, our best creative efforts, based on a broad awareness, would help us give American youth the aesthetic tools they need.

Art education as I understand it is multifaceted. Its content is drawing, painting, sculpture, etc.; it is design in its broad ramifications; it is art as historical impact, it is art criticism, it is *also* cultural communication. It requires the art of teaching based on highly developed understandings of individual

21

and cultural diversity and their relationship to learning. The art teacher can then *become* a central figure in cultural transmission and development.

Notes

[1]McFee, June K. *Preparation for Art*. Belmont: Wadsworth Publishing Co., 1961. Chapter XX.

[2]Gordon, Milton M. *Assimilation in American Life: The Role of Race, Religion, and National Origins*. New York: Oxford University Press, 1964, p. 51-54.

[3]*Ibid.*, p. 74-76.

[4]*Ibid.*, p. 34.

[5]*Ibid.*, p. 73.

[6]*Ibid.*, p. 254-257.

[7]Lee, Everett. "Internal Migration and Population Redistribution in the United States." Freedman, Ronald, ed. *Population: The Vital Revolution*. Garden City, NJ: Doubleday and Company, 1964.

[8]Berndt, Ronald and Catherine. *The First Australians*. New York: The Philosophical Library, 1954. p. 12.

[9]*Ibid.*, p. 104.

[10]*Ibid.*, p. 80.

[11]*Ibid* ., p. 75.

[12]Cook, Robert. Population Reference Bureau, Washington, D. C. Population Growth Symposium, Palm Springs, California, November 11, 1964.

[13]Statistical Abstract of the United States, 1964, 85th edition, "Metropolitan Growth."

[14]Churchill, Henry S. *The City Is The People*. New York: W. W. Nuton, Inc., 1962, pp. 198-202.

[15]Porter, Sylvia. "New Trends in Vocations" (Syndicated News Column), Prepublication Review of Darnell Corporation publication. New York, June 2, 1965.

[16]Brandwein, Seymour. *U. S. Dept. of Labor: Manpower, Automation and Training in Britannica Book of the Year 1964*. Chicago: Encyclopedia Britannica, Inc., p. 343.

[17]Loc, Cit., Cook.

[18]Helstein, Ralph; Piel, Gerald; Theobald, Robert. *Jobs, Machines, and People*. Santa Barbara: Center for the Study of Democratic Institutions, The Fund for the Republic, Inc., p. 15.

[19]Ibid., p. 20.

[20]Hoffman, Paul. "The Future of Mankind in a Shrinking World," *Views and Ideas on Mankind*. Council for the Study of Mankind, Bulletin No. 15; Dec., 1963, p. 2.

[21]Gould, Jack. *Television: One of a Series of Interviews on the American Character.* Santa Barbara: Center for the Study of Democratic Institutions, The Fund for the Republic, Inc., 1961, p. 3.

[22]*Ibid.*, pp. 4-6.

[23]McClosky, Herbert and Schaar, John H. "Psychological Dimensions of Anomy," *American Sociological Review, Vol. 30, No. 1*, Feb. 1965, p. 14-40.

Reprinted with permission from The Pennsylvania State University. From "Society, Art, and Education." Publication of *A Seminar for Research in Art Education*. 1966. Edward L. Mattil, Project Director and Editor. U.S. Office of Education Cooperative Project No. V-002. , pp. 122-140.

2

CULTURAL INFLUENCES ON AESTHETIC EXPERIENCE

INSEA Adelaide, Australia, 1978

The purpose of presenting this paper is to explore the complexities involved in viewing art cross-culturally. We need to find out what happens when people with one set of aesthetic values view art done by people with another set of aesthetic values. Philosophical theories of aesthetics are often based within a single cultural value system, so it is sometimes difficult to use a theory from one culture in responding to the work of an artist from a distinctly different culture.

But since one of our goals is to increase worldwide understanding through the arts, we also need to explore each other's aesthetic response to worldwide arts. For this reason we need to develop more awareness of the cultural factors that influence aesthetics.

There are contemporary philosophers who are concerned with cross-cultural aesthetics. Walter Abel searched for a unified interdisciplinary model for understanding aesthetics. He asserted that it is necessary to make a universal subject comprehensible to a given human being (Abel, 1952, p. 433). Melvin Rader and Bertram Jessup in their recent book *Art and Human Values* set the study of aesthetics in a much broader framework of inquiry (Rader & Jessup, 1976). It is set in a value context which can be compared cross-culturally. Rader and Jessup also open the traditional perimeters of art to include more of the artifacts used in human environments. Arnold Berleant in his theory of the aesthetic field identifies many of the variables that affect the aesthetic responses that are discussed here. Since my own inquiries in the arts are in the social and behavioral sciences I cannot assume to relate my inquiry to theirs as a philosopher might do.

This paper is focused on inquiry in two kinds of research: by *cultural anthropologists* who look at the variations in life ways and cultural patterns of people which may affect the aesthetic response; and by *experimental aestheticians* who look at both variability (differences in aesthetic response), and commonality (similarities in aesthetic response) among people everywhere. An exhaustive search of these fields is not claimed, but rather, an attempt is made to highlight studies which enable us to develop an overview model of recognising some of the complexities involved in looking at aesthetics cross-culturally. An overview is necessary if we wish to understand people's changing aesthetics perception in an age when the interchange of ideas and images has become almost instant through space-age electronic media. For this reason we need to be able to look at art from a cross-cultural perspective because we are being exposed to the arts that way. But, attempting such an overview is precarious because any specialists in any one aesthetic theory, or any student of any one culture will immediately identify factors that have been neglected in order to try to gain the broader perspective.

As educators in the arts we are concerned with how people develop aesthetic awareness, how their past experience affects how they experience works of art. We need to know how each society enculturates its young into using its own aesthetic view of reality. We also need to know what effect contemporary multicultural exposure is having upon aesthetic development. Further, we need to know how the values of a culture group tend to direct people's perceptual development. This will affect how students learn to perceive art. A simplistic view of aesthetic experience will not help us meet these educational challenges.

Definitions

The concept *culture* used in this paper refers to the values, attitudes and belief system of a group of people as they are manifested in human behaviour patterns, in the design of their art forms, and in the structure of their built environment. The concept *society* as used here means an organisation of a group of people who are held together for some purpose. INSEA, for example, is a society of people who are organised to promote education in the arts internationally. This is a social function. Though we share some cultural values about the arts and education we are not a homogeneous cultural group because we also represent varied cultural backgrounds. So the concepts society and culture have somewhat different meanings.

To discuss the *aesthetic experience* it would be helpful to have a working definition. But universal definition is difficult when the sense of what constitutes order, which underlies most aesthetic theory, varies widely from one part of the world to another. The Hindu sense of order and aesthetic experience is seen by the people as so integrated with life, that the anthropologist Richard Lannoy has used the history of the art of India as a keystone for describing its social organisation and value systems (Lannoy, 1971). By contrast, in more contemporary industrialized societies people tend to separate art and aesthetic experience in large degree from other aspects of life. Yet the ordering of the material aspects of the society functions as a central communication system in teaching and maintaining the value system. Much of this takes place through forms of art.

We have several strategies for trying to understand aesthetic experience cross-culturally. Firstly, we can search for universal or common denominators of cultural experience; secondly, we can use theories of aesthetics only with art created within the same cultural context to clearly assess this relationship as a basis for studying art in other cultures; thirdly, we can develop more understanding of the aesthetic values of many more cultural systems to increase our pool of cross-cultural aesthetic understandings; and fourthly, we can inquire how experience in a culture influences *what* people will learn to see and how they will see it. In educational language we can see how cultural experience in a group affects its members' abilities to respond aesthetically.

We need to work on all these options to understand the aesthetic experience when there are differences in values between the artist's culture and the viewer's culture. Thus we can enrich our understanding of diverse aesthetic experience as well as a diversity of art products.

Sources Of Cultural Differences

In a cross-cultural review of studies on perception of art, Miller asks a fundamental question: "...are these differences the result of differences in the ways in which cultural groups perceive the world in general, or are they the outcome of different cultures learning different conventions and techniques?" (Miller, 1973, p. 136). The work of Lannoy on India would strongly suggest that there are differences in ways of seeing the world, of organising it, and of depicting it (Lannoy, 1971).

Clifford Geertz, an anthropologist, writes that "The Western conception of the person as a rounded, unique, more or less integrated motivational and cognitive universe, a dynamic center of awareness, emotion, judgment and action..." separated from others and from nature is a "...peculiar idea within

27

the context of world cultures" (Geertz, 1975, p. 48). But it is within much of this cultural system that Western theories of aesthetics have evolved.

Geertz illustrates other cultural self-concepts where our traditional systems of aesthetics would be inadequate. The outside or observable for some Asian groups is the acceptable pattern of "external actions, movements, postures, speech", which are conceived of as essentially the same from one person to the next. Inward feelings by contrast are the emotional life of human beings accepted for all people. "It consists of the fuzzy shifting flow of subjective feeling perceived directly in all its phenomenological immediacy..." but considered to be "...identical across all individuals whose individuality it thus effaces" (Geertz, 1975, p. 49). It would appear that these people would consider that aesthetic experience would be the same for all people, while in societies stressing the uniqueness and separateness of the individual it is assumed that there is variability in the aesthetic response. But if people in different cultural groups have a different sense of self in relation to non-self, a different sense of inside-outside, then their reaction to art might vary accordingly.

Anthropologists have collected and recorded artifacts from groups all over the world, they have identified the similarities and differences in forms—but they have done little to record how the people judged the quality of the art forms, though they have long recognised that this needs to be done.

Certainly this aesthetic valuing of art which is handed down from generation to generation affects how new art is created. We could say that form follows cultural values as well as the function of the art form. Function and value are inextricably intertwined. Our cross-cultural study of aesthetics will be severely limited unless we can collect more evidence of the aesthetic valuing—the judging of the quality of art forms, in terms of the values of the persons creating them. When views of the world change, pressure is put on artists to change their art. Bohannan reported an example of this when an African Tiv schoolboy's criticism of his grandfather's carving caused the old man to change his work. The boy was learning standards of naturalism in art the grandfather did not share. This new world view put pressure on the old man to change his style (Bohannan, 1971, pp. 175-78).

It may not be possible to separate how much of a culture's art is the result of its people's world view, their aesthetic judgments, or from conventions or techniques they have evolved for depicting or expressing their experience. The techniques evolve as a means to express values. They are part of the environment in which children learn to see. As values change the techniques and the cultural values expressed change. People who grow up in culturally stable societies may have trouble responding to art from societies where culture is changing. Even within the same cultural group there are often sub-groups, adhering to or digressing from the traditions. This interferes with the aesthetic experience of people when either artist or viewer is in the other group.

Sub-Culture Of The Arts

We may also look at the values that develop among the people who communicate and develop each of the arts. Each art has evolved with different structures, organisations of parts, and different concepts used to describe their relationships. In other words, the cultural reality of music, drama, dance and art have evolved separately, but within a shared context, a value system milieu.

Even though we group the arts together as we do in this INSEA conference, we are apt to find more communication between musicians, between artists, or between dancers from different cultures than between people from the different arts working together. The reason may well be that at the operational level a group of people who make music, no matter what their sense of aesthetics, will have more in common, than they will with people who organise shapes and forms in two- and three-dimensional forms. They share forms and methods even though the meanings differ. When the concern shifts to symbols and meanings, the *media* grouping might break down and cultural groupings develop.

There is another cultural group in the world made up of those people who are part of an international network of people in the arts, who share the dominant themes in contemporary music, ballet, painting, and the theatre that ricochet around the world. Many of us are also members of this cultural group. So even if our own culture's art is different and our sense of aesthetics and reality quite different, we understand international styles and trends and can communicate at that level. This should not be confused with the need to understand each other's aesthetics because we may not share the same aesthetic response even though we are all responding to the same art.

Functions Of Art In Cultural Maintenance

To develop our overview of the aesthetic experience we need to begin with the functions of art in maintaining culture. We need to understand how people use art forms to maintain and transmit their cultural value systems. This is necessary because unless we understand this important cultural function we are missing part of art's meaning and our aesthetic response will be limited by this lack of knowledge.

The signs, symbols and design styles that have developed over time as familiar and associated with a group of people all have cultural reasons for being as they are. For example, art enhances a sense of group identity. One group is contrasted with another group by differences in the style of dress and design of ornamentation. Sex and age groups within the group are identified by variations of the group's style. Role and status within the group are also identified by further variation and extension of the design of costume, jewellery, and the ornament of objects. Often the more prestigious the role the more strongly is the message of importance carried through the design. The less prestigious are allowed to blend more easily with others like themselves. There are exceptions, of course, when people are of such greatness and so honored that they do not need the enhancement of costume to let others know who they are. The layout of cities and villages, and design of buildings, are expressions of what is valued in the society, what activities are given space to take place in, who goes on where, when and how, what is separated and what is connected, and what is excluded. But with all this ingroup variation there are often qualities of design that separate one cultural group from another.

Through art the concepts of reality, the meaning of the universe, the interpretation of the cycles of human life are made explicit (Gerbrands, 1957). The presence of this idea is felt, through expression in dance, music, theatre and the visual arts. The arts also enhance the quality of ritual carried on at critical points in human experience such as marriage, the change of leaders, or the harvest of food. Each group interprets these events through its art forms. For example, the symbolic meaning of the costuming, organisation of persons, music and ceremonial dance in the marriage ceremony are closely related to the accepted values about marriage and the relative roles of males and females. The social and economic status of the families is represented as well, and the degree of political power such a union will develop within a social group is expressed through the quality of the art forms used (McFee & Degge, 1977, pp. 272-93). The relationship of the institution of marriage to the cohesion of the social organisation is expressed through the art to show the importance given to the event. The importance of the religious values associated with marriage is expressed through the use of religious icons, which in turn express the concepts of the society in regard to natural law and the cosmos.

Depending on each of these variables the visual form of the marriage ceremony—the costuming, jewellery, pattern of movement of people, the identification of roles of different members of the marrying couple, the family, the society, and those given the power to perform the rite—all reflect the attitudes of the people in that cultural group. They are handed down from generation to generation and this continuity is preserved, in part, by the continued use of the art forms associated with it. The art provides the associations that give reality to the event.

In some societies this is very clear because the values are *widely accepted* and the culture is changing slowly. But in other societies culture change is rapid. Going back to our example of the marriage ceremony, great variability in dress, ceremonial dance and music is found in societies where the institution of marriage itself is changing, and the agreement on its relation to society and the traditional concepts of the natural order being reevaluated or questioned.

To understand art cross-culturally—to have an aesthetic experience beyond responding to the formal qualities of design (use of form, line, color and texture) one needs to understand how the art fits within the cultural value system, how it expresses specific qualities as seen by those people to maintain and enhance their culture. This cross-cultural understanding enhances our aesthetic experience in viewing their art (McFee & Degge, 1977, pp. 26-40).

Cross-Cultural Studies Of Perceptual Learning

Now I would like to turn to some of the cross-cultural studies that show differences in the ways people perceive as a result of their cultural experience. Such cultural effects would influence people's readiness to respond to art in their own and others' cultures. These studies are applicable to the visual arts, dance and some aspects of theatre.

Most of my illustrations are from the visual arts because that is the area I know most about. Similar examples of cross-cultural use of elements in the other arts should be analysed by persons from those fields.

Wayne Dennis has found that scores on the Draw-A-Man test decline among children from grade one to grade six, who are members of cultural groups where making images of the human figure is religiously unacceptable (Dennis, 1960). These scores do not mean the children regress from grades one to grade six but that they do not improve compared to the rate of children who have more opportunity to learn to see from drawings, paintings and photographs of people. It seems reasonable to assume that children and adults who grow up in societies with much—or little—visual imagery of the human figure will have different aesthetic experiences in viewing art works that include the human form.

Dennis, in later studies, found that children growing up in environments with complex visual imagery had higher scores on the Draw-A-Man test than those maturing in environments where the visual imagery was sparse (Dennis, 1966, pp. 213-15). As we look around the world and throughout the history of art the degree of variation in visual complexity is extensive. Thus the variations in the environments in which people learn to see and have aesthetic experience is extensive.

Differences in people's perceptions can only be inferred from the way they respond to different tasks. The ability to see cues of *depth perception* in photographs or drawings has been found to vary among cultural groups. This appears to be affected by opportunities that people have had to view two-dimensional surfaces that utilise the illusion of depth as a component. To what extent this is culturally learned behavior is not clear.

Miller finds that 'experience in seeing objects in the three-dimensional world is not sufficient to perceive those objects in pictorial representation' (Miller, 1973, p. 148). They need to see the representation of it. In an early study of Orotchen children, who were almost completely isolated from visual representation of any kind, they drew reindeer in three-dimensional perspective. Their survival depended on perception of reindeer which were the source of food, shelter and clothing (Schubert, 1930). The children could make pictorial representations from seeing objects. We can assume that they could recognise their own drawings. But this is quite different from seeing photographs of things where extraneous detail is not left out and one is not involved in making the image.

Another study of people raised in a distinct visual environment is reported by Turnbull who took some of his Pygmy friends out of the forest into the plains for the first time. Most of their visual experience with things was in a short focal distance. Their experience with large animals was only at close range because that was the only way they could be seen in the dense jungle. By contrast, the same animals a mile or so away in the plain were seen by them, as insects. They had not learned that things reduce in apparent size as they become more distant (Turnbull, 1962, pp. 260-65).

There is much to be resolved in settling the question of how people learn to see depth in pictorial representation. But for our purposes it is clear there are differences that result from opportunities to learn to see in nature and in pictures.

Cross-Cultural Differences in Perception Of Pictures

Recognising objects in pictures is only one aspect of the visual arts but considerable research has been undertaken to look for similarities and differences in this ability among people from different cultural backgrounds. Most of this work was done in Africa with different racial and cultural groups. There is continued controversy about the research design, but Miller, who has critically reviewed it, finds some generalisations that help us identify differences that may occur among cultural groups (Miller, 1973).

Object recognition in pictures apparently depends considerably on the amount of experience people have had in looking at pictures. Have they learned that a flat picture can represent three-dimensional objects? How familiar are they with the kinds of objects represented? For example, Zambian and Scottish children were compared in their recognition of animals and motor vehicles. The Scottish children could separate pictures of animals from machines more readily than the Zambian children. We assume the Scottish children had had more experience with machines and knew about animals from pictures and the Zambian children had less experience with machines and perhaps less experience with picture books of animals. Apparently, experience was a major factor in the differences in performance of these two groups. The Zambian children could more easily relate a picture of a hippopotamus to a model of one, whereas the Scottish children could better relate a picture of a pig to a model of one (Deregowski & Serpell, 1971). This indicates that familiarity with the subject helps one relate two- to three-dimensional reproductions of the same object. But if one is not familiar with the object it is more difficult to see the likenesses between the flat surface representation and the three-dimensional model.

Some evidence exists that persons who grow up where strict discipline of children is the norm see depth differently than do persons who grow up in societies where parents are more lenient. Furthermore, Dawson found differences within a culture. People's openness to new experience seems related to whether they were raised in *strict punitive* situations which made them more conforming and dependent, or *low punitive* situations which tended to make them more independent and non-conforming.

The *conforming people* were less open to new experiences and took longer to learn to use depth cues. The more open non-conforming people learned to use depth cues in pictures more quickly (Dawson, 1967). Different cultural values lead to different child-rearing practices and these affect the personality development of children which, in turn, affects how they learn to see depth in pictures. Thus, we have another cultural difference that needs to be considered in understanding aesthetic experience.

Certainly the art from different cultures varies in the amount and kind of depth cues used. The ability to perceive depth is much more important in learning to understand Western Renaissance art than in learning to understand Persian miniatures, for example. But any person walking around three-dimensional forms, or separating figure and ground in two-dimensional work is helped by having had experience in seeing some degree of depth in responding to art.

Another question to be considered is the degree to which different languages have concepts for dealing with visual imagery. Can people think about what they see if their language has few concepts for dealing with visual imagery? Certainly there is evidence that many people do think with visual images. But in what manner or to what extent this is affected by their language is still an open question. If the language does not have concepts for describing depth perception this affects the visual clues people seek. This selecting process then affects what they will perceive (DuToit, 1966).

Different peoples categorise color differently though there appear to be some basic commonalities around the world. The variations are mainly in the degree to which a single hue is differentiated, hardly at all in some societies and extensively in others. People with many words to describe variations in a color hue might respond to more variations in art than people who have learned to name only a few. Thus we might hypothesise that their aesthetic response to color will vary.

Effects Of Culture On Cognitive Styles

Jerome Bruner and his associates have made a cross-cultural study of children's problem-solving strategies, especially their use of visual cues or conceptual cues. They found two key trends: firstly, children who grow up in rural areas tend to use more perceptual cues; children in cities more words. In looking at something, a rural child would tend to tell you more about what it looked like, an urban child would tend to tell you the names of what he or she saw. Apparently the child who lives in a city, where there are so many cues, cannot deal with all the complexity and so abstracts it into name categories, whereas the rural child is not forced to abstract so much. Secondly, they found that children who grow up in some cultural groups tend to use *visual cues*, in others more *verbal cues*. This is related to the education the children receive, more conceptual or perceptual (Bruner, 1966). Remember that these are reports of central tendencies. Variations within groups—the ranges—also need to be studied.

I have tried to develop a model (Figure 1) that illustrates differences in ways people think and communicate (McFee & Degge, 1977, p. 335). Some people depend more on the left side of the diagram, using perceptualising and image-making abilities to learn and communicate, others more on the right, using conceptualising and verbalising abilities to learn and communicate. Although individuals differ in the use of one or the other mode they will also be affected by the values of their culture and the physical surroundings

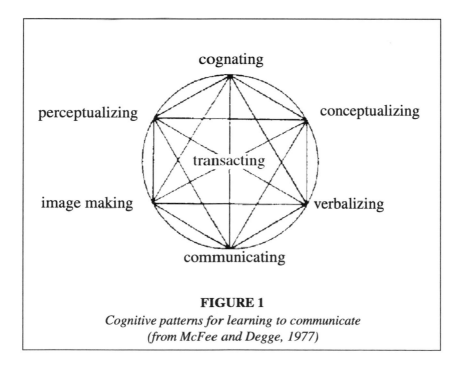

FIGURE 1

Cognitive patterns for learning to communicate
(from McFee and Degge, 1977)

they grow up in. Children who grow up in environments rich in art, where perceptual as well as conceptual training are stressed, where art as well as language is part of education, would probably develop in the categories on both sides of the diagram. I am not relating this to theories of left-right brain hemisphere, which would be premature, but rather to behaviours people evidence in their work.

But people who have developed any one of these modes of knowing and communicating, conceptual, perceptual, or both, would have a somewhat different aesthetic experience.

Cross-Cultural Commonalities

There is another perspective for looking at art culturally. Some psychologists concerned with experimental aesthetics are asking: What is there about human beings that has led to some kind of artistic production, and a regard for the aesthetic qualities in their environment, by all peoples in every culture? What is there in the structuring of art that is common to all people? What is common in the ordering processes that underlie the creation of the response to art? Is this parallel to the structuring of language, which though multifaceted in expression has commonalities in organisation?

Berlyne, a leader in the field of experimental aesthetics, reports that this inquiry, though a hundred years old, is still in its infancy. He defines the field as a study of the motivation effects of what he terms *collative* variables: *collative,* meaning how things are ordered or put together, *motivative,* meaning how the ordering of the work of art causes us to respond. He identified these motivating collative variables or ordering systems as 'variations along familiar-novel, expected-surprising, simple-complex, and clear-ambiguous dimensions' (Berlyne, 1972, p. 305).

Researchers are undertaking to study these dimensions cross-culturally in order to identify what part, if any, of the aesthetic experience is shared by all peoples and what part is idiosyncratic to people who share a common set of values. They have tentatively identified some commonalities.

The British psychologist H. J. Eysenck has been pursuing this idea for some years. In a recent study with Saburo Iwawaki he compared the preferences of 200 Japanese and 200 English students of both sexes. The two groups were of roughly the same age and intellectual standing. Neither group contained trained artists nor had the students had experience in the other culture.

The subjects rated 131 designs from Hornung's *Handbook* and they rated them from don't like, like a little bit, like, like a lot, and like very much (Hornung, 1932). Japanese and English, males and females, made quite similar judgments, though there was some difference between the sexes and the English of both sexes made more extreme judgments than the Japanese. Eysenck and Iwawaki feel that they have identified a commonality in aesthetic judgment in operation, in the subjects' ranking of these abstract designs (Eysenck & Iwawaki, 1975).

For some years I have been working with students to help them understand the processes of design and have used Figure 2 to help them identify factors that influence design. Any given aesthetic experience has cultural

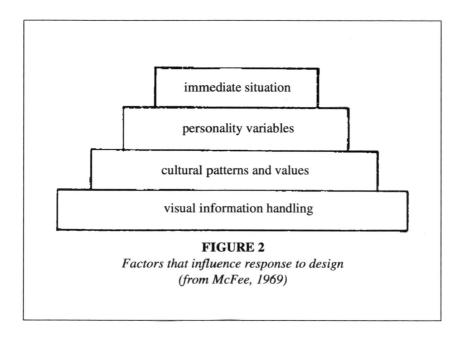

FIGURE 2
Factors that influence response to design
(from McFee, 1969)

factors, personality or readiness factors and it takes place in a given context which can change it.

We work at the level of basic information-handling processes using Gestalt concepts about similarity, proximity, and figure and ground, and continuity as a basis for creating order and variety through similar and different uses of the visual elements. This problem-solving process does not appear to be culture-bound. While it can be used to achieve the traditions of good aesthetics in the Western tradition of tensions and balance, it can also be used in cultures where balance, tension, contrast are not as important and art is more organismic, flowing, evolving.

Another art educator, Beverly Jones, has developed a model for identifying the main factors that influence art in a given culture (Figure 3). She posits that moral, religious, political and economic values interact with aesthetic value in the perception of any given art. A comprehensive understand-

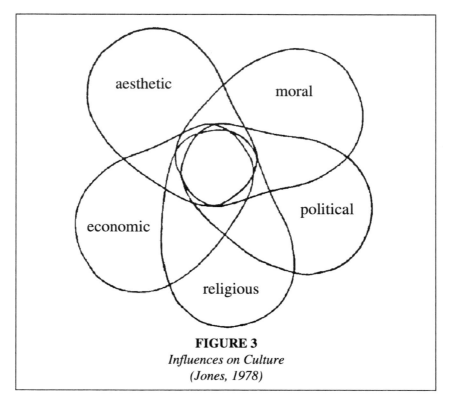

FIGURE 3
Influences on Culture
(Jones, 1978)

ing of the aesthetic response would include an awareness of the effect of all these influences. Jones's model cuts through one society to identify the variables within an individual's value structure that affect response to or creation of art at a given time. (Jones, 1978).

Summary

I have attempted to define aesthetic experience from a psychosocial-cultural, rather than a philosophical, context. I see it as transaction between the psycho-cultural readiness of the viewer to see, feel, understand, react, value and the composite of what is there to be responded to in the object, as it has evolved in reaction to or within the cultural tradition of the artist (Figure 4). The degree, nature, and quality of the aesthetic experience depends on the readiness and culture of the viewer, the quality and nature of the work and the degree of cultural congruence between the artist and the viewer. When we say that aesthetic experience cannot be separated from the cultural context in which it takes place we have to recognise that there are many levels with which to deal. A Western person viewing Eastern art, a Javanese viewing Balinese art, and a Balinese viewing Balinese art are three examples of different levels of communication: across wide traditions, between somewhat similar traditions and within traditions. Different levels also exist where social stratification or taste create different subcultures. Persons at each level will be able to have some transactional aesthetic experience but this experience will vary depending on the degree of similarity in cultural background of the viewer and the artist.

Some aspects of art can be experienced cross-culturally but this depends more upon the viewer's familiarity and responsiveness to art qualities than to his or her cultural background. People can have aesthetic experiences across cultural boundaries because there appear to be organisational modes, basic human processes of information handling that have some degree of universality. Aesthetically stimulating kinds of order and variety are found in all art; though people develop preferences for more or less variety and asymmetry depending on their culture. There are skills in the manipulation of media that can appeal to people's sense of fit between media, message and skill. There are qualities of art elements that appeal to us in myriad forms, though most cultures emphasise some but not others. There are universals of message about the human condition that we can identify with—and to the degree that we know something about the values and belief systems of other cultures

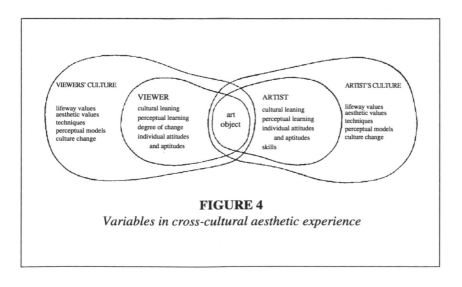

FIGURE 4

Variables in cross-cultural aesthetic experience

we can react to their art in terms of our degree of understanding of that culture.

Viewers from the same culture with similar art sensitivities will have similar aesthetic transactions with art forms from their own cultural background. They will experience the iconography, the ways structures and form are developed, the way space is used and symbolised, qualities of their culture's mode of transacting with the outside world that other people may not comprehend.

The questions that this perspective raises for me relate to whether a comprehensive cross-cultural aesthetics is possible, and whether there are some aspects of art that are universal, or is this only a Western perspective? Is the international art-apprehending group a subculture made up of people around the world from various cultures who, through exposure and response to the visual arts, have developed sensitivities that enable them to have a somewhat similar aesthetic experience?

Even among such sensitive people there probably have developed different modes of attending to art depending on personality, experience and culture; some may be more perceptual, some more conceptual, some more affective, some more analytical, some concerned with formalism, some with emotional impact, and yet all attend to qualities in art, as we have seen. The environment people grow up in, which of course is highly influenced by culture, also affects how generally sensitive to art people will become.

What this seems to be saying is that aesthetic experience from a cross-cultural perspective depends on a person's individual perceptual-conceptual development, the kind of visual environment in which he or she has grown up—the way he or she learns to see and think, the imagery in the environment in which he or she has learned to see, which supports and enhances the sense of cultural identity, the sense of cosmic reality, the systems for judging art, the understanding of societal structure, and the meaning of life.

To help children and young people learn to understand other people's art we have to expose them to far more than the art object or event itself. They need a rich understanding of all the cultural factors that help the artist give it form. Perhaps this deeper understanding of each other's aesthetic experience in evaluating and responding to art will give us greater insights and understandings of peoples around the world.

If this is so it behooves us to accelerate the task of filling the great gaps in our knowledge of what constitutes aesthetic experience among the arts as well as between peoples if we are to more fully understand the functions of the arts in human society and life.

References

Abel, W. (1952). Toward a unified field in aesthetics. *Journal of Aesthetics and Art Criticism, 10*(3), March.

Berleant, A. (1970). *The aesthetic field.* Springfield, IL: Charles C. Thomas.

Berlyne, D. E. (1972). Ends and means of experimental aesthetics. *Canadian Journal of Aesthetics, 26*, pp. 303-42.

Bohannan, P. (1971). The artist in tribal society. In C. M. Otten (Ed.), *Anthropology and Art.* New York: Natural History Press.

Bruner, J. S. (1966). *Studies in Cognitive Growth.* New York: John Wiley.

Dawson, J. I. M. (1967) Cultural and physiological influences upon spatial-perceptual process in West Africa —Part I. *International Journal of Psychology, 2*, pp. 115-28.

Dennis, W. (1960). The human figure drawings of bedouins. *Journal of Social Psychology, 52*, pp. 209-19.

Dennis, W. (1966). Goodenough scores, art experience and modernization. *Journal of Social Psychology, 68*, pp. 213-15.

Deregowski, J., & Serpell, R. (1971). Performance on a sorting task with various modes of representation: A cross-cultural experiment. *Human Development Research Units Reports* (University of Zambia) No. 18.

DuToit, B. M. (1966). Pictorial depth perception and linguistic relativity. *Psychologia Africana II*: pp. 51-63.

Eysenck, H. J., & Iwawaki, S. (1975). The determination of aesthetic judgment by race and sex. *The Journal of Social Psychology 96*(1), June, pp. 11-20.

Gertz, C. (1975). On the nature of anthropological understanding. *American Scientist, 63*(1), pp. 48-9.

Gerbrands, A. A. (1957). *Art as an element of culture especially in Negro Africa.* E. J. Brill, Leiden.

Hornung, C. P. (1932). *Handbook of design and devices.* London: Harper.

Jones, B. (1978) Unpublished research. University of Oregon.

Lannoy, R. (1971). *The speaking tree.* London: Oxford University Press.

McFee, J. K. (1969). Visual communication. In R. V. Wiman & W. C. Mierhenry, (Eds.), *Educational media: Theory into practice*, pp. 195-216. Columbus, OH: Charles E. Merrill Books, Columbus.

McFee, J. K. (1970). *Preparation for art*, 2nd ed. Belmont, CA: Wadsworth.

McFee, J. K., & Degge, R. M. (1977). *Art, culture and environment.* Belmont, CA: Wadsworth.

Miller, R. J. (1973). Cross-cultural research in the perception of pictorial materials. *Psychological Bulletin, 80*(2), p. 136.

Rader, M., & Jessup, B. (1976). *Art and human values*. Englewood Cliffs, NJ: Prentice-Hall.

Schubert, A. (1930). Drawings of Orotchen children and young people. *Journal of Genetic Psychology, 37*, pp. 232-34.

Turnbull, C. (1962). *The forest people*. New York: Doubleday.

Reprinted with permission of Holt, Rinehart and Winston. From "Cultural Influences on Aesthetic Experience" in Proceedings *The International Society for Education Through Art*. 23rd World Congress, Sydney, Australia. 1980.

3

CROSS-CULTURAL INQUIRY INTO THE SOCIAL MEANING OF ART: IMPLICATIONS FOR ART EDUCATION

CSEA/USSEA Conference, Vancouver, 1986

Dear Friends, what a joy it is to meet with you again. You are here because you selected to come to a conference on exploring the futures of art and culture. It means to me that your concerns are worldwide and your interests in art and education are multi-cultural, not ethno-centric.

And what a privilege we all have to meet together in this magnificent city—a crown among cities everywhere. I have been visiting this place for well over half a century so have some sense of its development. In the interim, we have lived and studied as cities, Sydney and Perth, Australia, Singapore and London as well as lived or frequently visited many in North American and some in Europe. Each has greatness in its own unique way.

But Vancouver's combinations of attributes sets it apart from all the rest. It has an intense yet disciplined vitality built from the complex of cultures of the people and their values that came to this magnificent mountain and sea site.

They have created a very contemporary, yet humane and historical place, for people of many cultures to be. It has deep roots transferred not only from England but also by people from the Empire, now the Commonwealth, and the rest of the world. It has not lost its ties with the indigenous people and their art that helps define the nature of the place. It has maintained in large part its respect for the power of the landscape.

To me it is a showplace for the future as the population of the world becomes more interrelated. Expo 86 will surely draw you, but don't neglect to see this urban art form, of which the exposition is but a landmark in its remarkable development.

Let me add another note about Canada. A recent newspaper article on Manitoba is symptomatic of North America as a whole. In that province there are 55 ethnic groups represented. Less than half the population have English or French speaking backgrounds. There are evening and weekend classes in twenty other languages (*Christian Science Monitor*, 5/6, 1986. p. 11). In greater or lesser degree, we are all becoming more multicultural. Thus the need for cultural understanding between groups is both within and among societies.

In the past art educators have depended mainly on anthropology for its foundation for cross-cultural study. Other fields have been addressing this need as well, and in some cases have useful theory and research for us. These include cross-cultural psychology, cross-cultural training, which is a field of education for people preparing to work in cultures other than their own, trans-cultural psychiatry, which compares emotional and personality trends, the comprehensive field of folk art, cross-cultural and experimental aesthetics, cross-cultural communication and our own subfield cross-cultural art education. This body of work is becoming a resource of its own. INSEA and its regional affiliates, the Social Theory Caucus of the NAEA, the growing number of dissertations, the research of individuals as evidenced at this conference, all contribute papers to this field. (McFee, 1988)

After much reflection, I decided that the most fruitful contribution I could make to this conference was to analyze definitions of our key words *art* and *culture,* as they have been developed, and are now used, in anthropology, cross-cultural psychology, and cross-cultural training. Concepts with such rich dimensions have implications for us.

A word of caution is due here—It is almost impossible for me to separate the words *art* and *culture,* though I will focus first on art and then culture.

Art

Melville Herskovits in 1959 summarized previous definitions and descriptions of art based on anthropologists' field work. He makes several points:

1. "To be classified as an object of art ... [the object] must meet cultural criteria of form" (Herskovits, 1955, p. 46). For us to appreciate the art, we need to understand the cultural criteria.

2. "...What a people consider surpassingly pleasing, beauty as an abstraction, is broadly spread over the earth, and lies deep in human experience" (Herskovits, 1959, p. 43). It is important to note that he is saying there is a universal need for what is culturally pleasing. He is not saying there is a universal beauty. This question is still debatable.

3. "... Every people, in every age has poor artists as well as good" (Herskovits, 1959, p. 47).

4. Herskovits stresses that artistic expression is universal in terms of societies, but that every individual in a society does not function as a culturally defined artist and that among these, there are varieties in performance.

5. Finally, he stresses that "... art is a cultural phenomenon, ... its appreciation is best gained through the broadest possible understanding of the cultural matrix out of which it comes" (Herskovits, 1959, p. 59).

I believe we can reverse this and also say that culture is maintained, transmitted and changed through art; its appreciation can be largely enhanced by understanding all its art.

Herskovits deplored the study of art without knowledge of its context. Such led us in Western societies to put the art from so called "civilized" countries in art museums where the artist's identity is stressed and so called "uncivilized" people's art in natural history museums where the individual artist was mainly ignored (Herskovits, 1959, p. 55).

This challenges us to become increasingly aware of the ways we have been programmed to view art as we respond to the art of other cultures. Not only are we challenged to try to comprehend the values of the other culture, but we need to recognize the screen through which we are seeing and thinking about it.

Let me give you an example. A middle-class college educated California woman with self-recognized lack of knowledge about art went to the Louvre for the first time. Curious about her reactions, I asked her that night what had impressed her. Among her remarks, she said she was disappointed in the Venus de Milo. Asked why, she said, "Well I didn't like her Roman nose." Her embeddedness in her own culture—with its collective values on facial physiognomy, her lack of exposure to even classic art, or Greco-Roman history, restricted her response.

Clifford Geertz, in analyzing the place of art in culture, proposes that art is more than a symbol to transmit meaning. It is itself semiotic, a mode of making meaning. Artists learn in some degree their modes of thought from

45

their culture, and their work is created to be responded to by people who share the same cultural modes of knowing and seeing.

He describes the basic factors in the arts as those activities which give *visible, audible,* and what he calls *tactible* form to ideas so that we can respond with our senses and emotions and then reflect or think about our response (Geertz, 1983, pp. 119-120). In other words, art is a mode of knowing as well as communicating.

Chalmers and others have identified some of the ways art functions to identify cultural values, belief systems, status and roles, ways of making order. (Chalmers, 1973, 1980; McFee and Degge, 1980, pp. 272-297).

Using this material, I would like to propose the following outline for describing the functions of art.

1. The art of *objectification* is used to make subjective values, emotions, ideas, beliefs, superstitions more sensually tangible. They can be seen and felt.
2. The art of *enhancement* is used to enrich celebration and ritual of human events, to express quality, character, kind. The nature of being and of events is expressed in the nature of design.
3. The art of *differentiation* is used to identify categories and variations in types.
4. The art of *organization* is used to illustrate structures and the culturally accepted relations of parts and the meanings of wholes.
5. The art of *communication* is used to record, transmit and generate, meanings, qualities and ideas.
6. The art of *continuity* is used to stabilize culture, to perpetuate the convictions of reality, the identities and accomplishments of individuals and groups.
7. The art of *culture change* leading or documenting ways values, attitudes, and belief systems are changing.

These art functions operate individually, in combinations, and in varying degrees, throughout the human produced culture, affecting the experience of people subjectively and objectively.

We can apply these functions of art in analyzing what we Westerns call fine art, crafts, folk art, ethnic art, indigenous art, artifacts, architecture, habitats, settlement patterns, costume, landscapes, etcetera, to objectify, enhance, differentiate, organize, communicate, and continue culture.

Culture

The concept *culture* has two kinds of meanings. The English word is derived from the Latin meaning for preparing and maintaining soil so plants would grow. The historical tradition of applying this to the cultivation of the mind and taste to more "civilized" Western European standards is very different from that used by the social sciences in which all peoples are seen to have values, attitudes and belief systems which they share in part with their own cultural group.

Hofstede puts it succinctly "to say, 'he/she has no culture' is almost as bad as 'he/she has no personality" (Hofstede, 1984, p. 21).

The two uses of the word are not always kept clear in art education. If we use the elitist historical meaning of culture, we assume our own quality criteria are the only bases for judging any art and miss much of its meaning. If we use the social science meaning we must not neglect the consideration of differences in quality within a cultural group's art—while at the same time seeing each culture's art as relative to its own quality criteria.

In 1951, Kluckhohn summarized the definitions of culture as used by anthropologists up to that time. This definition is still quoted today by people in different fields, as its central meaning.

"Culture consists in patterned ways of thinking, feeling and reacting, acquired and transmitted mainly by symbols, constituting the distinctive achievement of human groups, including their embodiment in artifacts; the essential core of culture consists of traditional (i.e., historically derived and selected) ideas and...their attached values" (Kluckhohn, 1951, p. 5).

The contemporary anthropologist Clifford Geertz denotes culture as "an historically transmitted pattern of meanings embodied in...inherited conceptions expressed in symbolic form by means of which men [and women] communicate, perpetuate and develop their knowledge about and attitudes towards life" (Geertz, 1983, p. 89).

We recognize that art, architecture, and the design of cities are in large part objective symbols of cultural patterns and meanings. They are symbolic modes of thought using art as the language (McFee, in press).

Ten years later Geertz cautions us in his essay on the current state of social theory. He states that "we are all natives" trying to find out how others, "across the sea or down the corridor organize their significant world" Geertz, 1983, p. 151). He points out that there are many diverse theories in the social sciences about how different peoples think—how others differ from us. If we assume we are superior, we tend to look for ways others are inferior. If we assume all humankind equal, we tend to neglect the variations and uniqueness among them.

Geertz further points out the importance of recognizing the differences in how people define themselves as persons from one culture to another. From the standpoint of a separate and unique sense of self in some societies, it is hard to recognize the sense of self that is more integrated into the flux and flow of their social group (Geertz, 1983, pp. 58-59).

Brislin, a cross-cultural psychologist, cautions us about cultural ethnocentrism. He stresses that a society's cultural symbols themselves, as well as their meanings, are valued—particularly symbols of subjective beliefs and ideologies. The symbol becomes a way to value them. Our symbols tend to have more meaning to us than others do, thus we value other symbols less (Brislin, 1983, p. 367).

Geert Hofstede, a Dutch cross-cultural psychologist, writing in his anthropologically based book, *Cultures Consequences, International Differences in Work Related Values*, defines culture as, "...the interactive aggregate of common characteristics that influenced a human group's response to its environment. Culture determines the identity of a human group [in similar ways] ...as personality determines [helps identify] an individual." It is "... the collective programming of the mind which distinguishes the members of one human group from another. This is identified by behavior" (Hofstede, 1984, p. 21).

He identifies three levels of mental programming; *universal*, shared by almost all humans, *collective*, those we have learned in a cultural group, and *individual*, the unique way of individuals (Hofstede, 1984, pp. 14-15).

This analysis of Hofstede helps us begin to question in our own thought those concepts that are universals, that are culturally collective, and that may be our own. All these may be operative when we make cross-cultural responses to art.

Triandis, a cross-cultural psychologist, compares his work to anthropologists who focus more on the culture of the group. Psychologists start with attributes of individual people to identify the culture as a whole. But Triandis believes that a great deal of study as an anthropologist is needed to understand the cultural patterns before study of the individual is undertaken. He finds both methods necessary for a more complete understanding of human culture to be achieved. He also identifies two aspects of culture:

1. *"Objective elements,"* such as the ways people in a culture use space, the tools they invent, the objects they make.

2. *"Subjective elements,"* such as what they consider to be normal, what they value and the hierarchy of values, and the ways they divide up the thing that must be done into different roles (Triandis, 1983, p. 82).

I would suggest that art operates in both of these aspects. Art has an objective element even if only momentary as in a happening. It may have centuries of cultural influence through the settlement pattern of ancient cities, whose builders' subjective values concerning space relations still influence how the sites are objectively used today. In most objective aspects of art and artifacts (human-made objects) subjective cultural elements are to be found.

Triandis has identified key ways in which individuals can prepare themselves to be able to function in another culture. I have adapted these to comprehending the role of art and the artist in another culture. These include norms, roles, values and expectations of the members of a cultural group toward their art and artists (Triandis, 1983, p. 85).

What are the norms for artistic behavior, who does what, when and how?

What is the relationship of the artist to the rest of the group?

What are the ways the artist expresses the general intentions of the group?

How does a given artist's self-concept compare to the norms for other people in the group?

What values are clearly accepted or rejected in and through their art?

What are the group's beliefs about art's antecedents and consequences? What is art based on? What effects is it expected to have? How much variation in artistic behavior is tolerated? How should the artist be rewarded?

If we look at just the art and not these norms, roles, values and expectations that affect the artist, we miss much of the meaning. We are so prone to ask, "What did the artist mean? What was the artist's message?" To even begin to comprehend the artist's meaning, we must also know the cultural factors that have given rise to that artist's sense of self, the motivations, the cultural patterns for art and the rewards to create a particular type of art. Another aspect of variation we need to attend to is the ways people learn to see, what they attend to, what organizing systems they use for sorting and organizing visual information in different cultures (McFee, 1980, pp. 45-52).

Degregowski, a cross-cultural psychologist specializing in perception, points out that their studies in this area generally have been looked at with Western theories of perception (Degregowski, 1980, pp. 21-115). But a large number of studies have been done usually indicating differences in perception of pictures, response to illusions, to the constancies, (that is, apprehending things as they are known to be rather than as they appear in the retinal image), response to geometric patterns, symmetry and asymmetry, perception of color and form. Differences in all these ways of attending will affect the art produced by a given people (McFee, Degge, 1980, pp. 94-107).

Another whole body of research and practice has grown up since the beginning of the Peace Corps in what is called *cross-cultural training*. Several methods were tried but the most successful were those that combined cognitive understanding of another culture with the more important humbling understanding of oneself as a product of culture, in order to communicate with people whose cultural learning has been different (Page and Martin, 1983, p. 41).

In a summary of the most useful abilities needed by people working in international situations, Page and Martin list "the ability to tolerate ambiguity, empathy, the ability to withhold judgment, reduction of ethno-centrism, a culturally relativistic world view, an appreciation of other values and belief systems, personal flexibility, a willingness to acquire new patterns of behavior and belief" (Page and Martin, 1983, pp. 43-44).

We've had a long history of colonial and missionary encounters where indigenous people were looked upon as children. We encouraged them to accept our systems of law and religious belief but we didn't ask them in for tea. The abilities recognized now as needed for cross-cultural work were not considered vital. These abilities are also needed to see others' art as not childlike or of lesser value just because its cultural context is different.

Further, the tendency still prevailed in the Western mind and among those with Judeo-Christian traditions that differences among themselves are minor compared to the rest of the world. The cross-cultural psychologists are now carrying on where the national character studies of the 40s and 50s left off. They are doing cross-cultural psychological testing in this part of the world as well as others.

I would like to report to you a study by Hofstede that illustrates the cultural diversity within the Western tradition on just one item—the sources of motivation (Hofstede, 1984, p. 259). This study suggests that in Great Britain and their former dominions and colonies, including Canada and the United States, the dominant source of motivation is the need for "personal," individual success. In German speaking countries and Greece, it is the need for individual security. In France, Spain, Portugal and Yugoslavia, it is the need for security and group solidarity. In Northern European countries, plus the Netherlands, it is for collective success and belonging, and the living environment.

Each of these needs is culturally developed, though individuals in each group will vary. There seem to be tendencies towards these different sources of motivation in the different national groups.

Up to this point, we have been describing culture and the elements that different thinkers have identified as part of it. We must also realize that each of these elements are not static but are in process. Some anthropologists have shifted from the use of the concept culture change which infers a static condition that changes to think of culture as a socio-cultural system. Richard Handler points out that "the elements, events and aspects" of these systems are in constant change, yet at the same time persist (Handler, 1984, p. 56). Any element of the system is taking on emergent qualities yet relates to past elements. In a way, it's like the old parlour game where a message is whispered from one person to another going around a circle. The message at its start is related to the message at the end but has been modified by most who transfer it.

This same analysis can be applied to art. We can identify the art of a cultural group yet still find variety and emerging trends in it. While we look for describable qualities, these are always in transition.

Now we will summarize. As we do so, remember the two concepts, culture and art, are processes with tendencies to persist yet with emerging qualities or aspects.

The culture of a group of people includes the patterned ways they have learned:
- To think, believe, feel, value, react, see, sort and order.
- To identify and relate the self to the group.
- To accept roles and divide up work, play and art.
- To cope with their environment.
- To create their human-built environment.
- To react to their human-built and natural environment.
- To change and modify their culture.

Culture is learned, transmitted, maintained and modified through language, behavior, ritual, play and art.

51

Culture has objective, subjective, universal, collective and individual dimensions.

To be effective in cross-cultural teaching and in responding to art, we need to become more aware of our own culture patterning, less ethno-centric, less judgmental from our cultural perspectives, more flexible and empathetic with others, as well as [to] develop our cognitive understanding of them.

Art as defined in the social sciences may be described as the processes and products of individual artists, who are in a state of moving towards or away from their culture's central modes of thought, of acceptable emotions, of hierarchy of values, of symbolic, stylistic productive tradition, and systems for making order. Art is a mode or knowing as well as communicating

The artwork, as object, stimulates in respondents subjective visual, emotional, intuitive, as well as reasoned modes of thought depending upon the viewers individual aptitudes and culturally learned abilities and values.

Art objectifies, enhances, differentiates, organizes, communicates and gives continuity to culture. Culture gives meaning and structure.

It seems very clear at this point that culture and art cannot be discussed separately. If we ignore the impact of art upon culture, we cut out one of the central means for transmitting, organizing, and learning culture. If we leave the understanding of culture out of art, we get only culture centric, limited, biased and often erroneous messages from it.

What are the implications of this for use at this conference and in the future? Let me briefly suggest a few.

First of all we need much more research on art in its cultural context to develop materials for teaching or to direct students' inquiry:

1. What are the cultural influences on the creation of a given group's art?
2. How does the art reflect that culture?
3. How does art enhance and transmit cultural values, qualities, attitudes, beliefs and roles?
4. What are the criteria for judging art?
5. What are the emergent qualities in art and the culture?
6. What is the role of the artist in the culture?
7. How does an individual learn to be an artist?
8. Where does a given artist fit within the cultural group?

We also need much more research on the cultural adaptations of different groups within and entering our societies and the relation of art to those cultures.

We need a broader base of social foundations of art education to include cross-cultural psychology and training, folk art theory, cross-cultural aesthetics, etc., as well as our anthropological basis. This is needed for graduate study and teacher training.

All this foundational work also needs to be translated into curricular materials that can be used with students to help them study art in its cultural context and to see how art helps maintain and sometimes change cultural values and beliefs. A range of specific art and culture studies need to be presented to help them understand art cross-culturally and begin to grasp the impact of their own culture on their own art.

We've gotten some help from the cross-cultural training psychologists in identifying the flexibility and openness of mind needed by all of us whether in cross-cultural research, teaching art in cross-cultural situations, or in apprehending art from cultures other than our own.

We need to analyze our teaching methods and practices to see if they encourage the development of the flexible attributes to respond to art cross-culturally.

Finally, we need to bring ourselves up to date in our own field. What have art educators done to date in cross-cultural analysis of art, of teaching art, and of students in cross-cultural situations. We need to analyze their research methods and the quality of their research. We need to find out which research techniques make them comparable. The reports given at this conference will be a major contribution to this literature for we need a critical assessment of what it may mean as a body of knowledge and how it fits with the materials from the other related fields.

References

Brislin, R. W (1983). Cross-cultural research in psychology. *Annual Review of Psychology, 34*, pp. 363-400.

Chalmers, G. F. (1980). The art of contemporary "tribes." Using the methods or cultural anthropology to study the out-of-school arts of our students. In J. Conders, J. Howlett and J. Skull (Eds.), *Arts in cultural diversity: INSEA 23rd world congress.* Sydney, New York, Toronto, & London: Holt, Rinehart & Winston, pp. 128-132.

Chalmers, G. F. (1973). The study or art in a cultural context. *Journal of Aesthetics and Art Criticism, 32*, pp. 249-256.

Geertz, C. (1983). *Local knowledge.* New York: Basic Books, p. 244.

Geertz, C. (1973). Thick description: Toward an interpretive theory of culture. In C. Geertz, *The interpretation of cultures.* New York: Basic Books, p. 470.

Handler, R. (1984). On socio-cultural discontinuity: National and cultural objectification in Quebec. *Current Anthropology*, pp. 25:56.

Herskovits, M. J. (1959). Art and value. In Redfield, R., Herskovits, M. J., and Ekholm, G. F., *Aspects of primitive art.* New York: The Museum of Primitive Art, p. 100.

Hofstede, G. (1984). Cultures consequences: International dIfferences in work-related values. Vol. 5, *Cross-Cultural Research and Methodology Series*, Beverly Hills: Sage Publications, p. 325

Kluckhohn, C. (1951). The study of culture. In D. Lerner, and H. D. Lasswell (Eds.), *The Policy Sciences.* Stanford, CA: Stanford University Press, p. 86.

McFee, J. K. (1980). Cultural influences on aesthetic experiences. In J. Conders, J. Howlett and J. Skull (Eds.), *Arts in cultural diversity: INSEA 23rd world congresss.* Sydney, New York, Toronto & London: Holt, Rinehart & Winston, pp. 45-52.

McFee, J. K. (1988). Cultural dimensions in the teaching of art. In F. H. Farley, R. W. Neperud (Eds.), *The Foundation of Aesthetics, Art and Art Education.* New York: Praeger.

McFee, J. K. and Degge, R. M. (1980). *Art, culture and environment.* Dubuque: Kendall/Hunt, p. 398.

Paige, R. M. and Martin, J. M. (1983). Ethical issues and ethics in cross-cultural training. In D. Landis and R. W. Brislin (Eds.). *Handbook of intercultural training. Vol. I Issues of theory and design*, pp. 36-60.

Triandis, Harry C. (1983). Essentials of studying cultures. In D. Landis and R. W. Brislin (Eds.). *Handbook of intercultural training. Vol. I, Issues of theory and design.* pp. 82-117.

Newspapers

The *Christian Science Monito*r. May 5, 1986, p. 11.

Selected Other Readings

Anderson, F. E. (1979). Approaches to cross-cultural research in art. *Studies in Art Education*, 21(1) pp. 17-25.

Boyer, B. (In Press). Cross-cultural studies in aesthetic behavior with implications for art education. *Visual Arts Research.*

Congdon, K. G. (1984). A folkloric approach for teaching folk art: Benefit for cultural awareness. *Journal of Multi-Cultural and Cross-Cultural Research in Art Education*, 2(1), pp. 5-13.

Jones, B. J. and McFee, J. K. (1986). Research in teaching arts and aesthetics. In E. C. Whitrock (Ed.). *Handbook of Research on Teaching, Third Edition. A Project of the American Educational Research Association.* New York: Macmillan Publishing Company, pp. 906-916.

Reprinted by permission. From "Cross Cultural Inquiry into the Social Meaning of Art: Implications for Art Education." Proceedings at the CSEA/USSEA Conference Exploring Cultural Backgrounds, Exploring Cultural Futures, University of British Columbia, 1986. *Journal of Multi-cultural and Cross-cultural Research in Art Education*, 1986, 4:1 pp. 6-16.

4

CULTURAL DIVERSITY AND CHANGE: IMPLICATIONS FOR ART EDUCATION

Fellows Symposium NAEA, Kansas City, 1990

In this presentation we will analyze some of the factors in culture change and diversity in contemporary American society that are affecting art, and art education (McFee, 1988 and 1995). But before doing this we need to establish a bench mark of art in American society before considering change.

First, we must recognize that we have a culture bound, Western system of defining, categorizing, rating, socially stratifying, and responding to art. *Second*, that within a complex cultural system such as ours there are many subcultures; some perceived as having more status or value than others. Each has its own variations of art, expressing that subcultures' values and acceptable styles. Most groups have typical artists whose work can be contrasted with work of artists in other subcultures, such as those who create "pop" contrasted with "folk" art. French anthropologist, Pierre Bourdieu has done an extensive study of his country's stratification of the visual arts within different socioeconomic classes, each with its subcultural variations in aesthetics, and styles, and each using art to define group identity and social status (Bourdieu, 1984).

Our country has prided itself in being less stratified and a more open society. While much upward mobility actually occurs, two new factors raise questions about our openness. *First*, is the recent recognition that we may have an underclass, whose members have little chance of improving their status. *Second* is the general trend of a majority of young people being unable to achieve beyond their parents' lifestyle and social status. This leads us to ask if those cultural mores called "The American Dream" are being undermined. We are all familiar with upward mobility influencing people's taste in the art forms they think they need to acquire. But learning to live with less through better design has not had high priority. Within our upward and onward cultural value system education for downward mobility has rarely been considered. But environmental factors, the need to conserve energy, space and resources will require a leaner sense of design by all social groups.

Because people share a large overall culture does not mean that all of the people understand all its parts. Few can respond to the arts of all its subcultures. Perhaps the Warhol phenomenon had such impact because he broke through traditional hierarchies of what was acceptable art within the different subcultures. The recent political fanfare about what is acceptable as art is that a politician tried to put his subcultural definition of art on all public supported creation and exhibition of art. This was interpreted as defining art for the public, and thus limiting freedom of artistic expression. But the fact that the public is composed of multiple subcultures of varied values and attitudes about art was not recognized.

Now we will look at some changes in the so-called dominant society that affect the ways people live their lives and with their art.

First, are factors that surround the changing roles of women. At the same time that more mothers are working than are staying at home, there are also far more women with small children living in poverty. Both of these factors decrease women's time for creative work and contributing to the vast networks that support the arts. This change in women's roles can affect the way future generations value art, and the kinds of life styles developed when there is less time for art. After our decades of trying to democratize the arts they may now become more elitist unless through education we can show their applicability to multiple life styles, and time restrictions.

Second, are changes in the usage of space in much of the country. As population, inflation, and loss of low income housing increases more people are having to live in less space than ever before. Art will need to be designed to function within this smaller social and physical context no matter whether it is fine, folk, or popular art, or whether it is housing, product, or environmental design.

Third, reductions in national and state support for the arts and the current wrenching struggle to prioritize our national needs among urban, educational, and social network requirements at home and unprecedented demands abroad will influence the support and practice of the arts in education, and in society.

58

It is a distressing paradox that in the political response to President Bush's State of the Union Address in February of 1990 no one went *beyond* his call for better math and science education. The critical need for wisdom in using them to serve humanity was not addressed. This requires study of the quality of urban and rural living space, of social change, of increasing cultural diversity. The needs of the family, basic human rights and institutions in this country, need to be studied through the arts, social ecology, social sciences, and humanities. If this balance is not achieved we could excel in producing new products but lack skills in knowing their social and environmental costs. With moves towards democracy changing much of the world the citizens of established democracies need to sharpen their humane and design skills, as well as science and math, to maintain cultures in which democracy can flourish.

Fourth, is the impact of television on culture, starting with the socialization of children into the culture it projects.

Recently we recognized the increased pace and sensationalism used to hold viewers' attention to keep people from double viewing, program scanning and avoiding what is advertised. But have we recognized that programs as well as advertising are used to create a deep seated "need to buy" mentality—a new cultural norm. Schiller reviews and analyzes the impact of the use of television to subvert people's value systems to a consumer culture. His book, *Culture Inc.*, shows the control of the flow of information and its effect on individual freedom of choice (Schiller, 1989). These values and choosing behaviors are molded to serve economic demands made from corporate decisions. They do not grow out of usual cultural development where values and behavior norms are shared, and transmitted to serve the living patterns of a group of people.

To understand cultural influences on children, the images that have meaning to them, and the styles of interaction and transition that they have internalized, we must be aware of the mass corporate culture that they are exposed to, with its selection of what is of value, its criteria of how choices should be made and the styles of visual imagery used to project them.

Fifth, we need to discuss, one of our most challenging changes—to educate the children from cultures around the world that are pouring into our schools. If they were entering a stable, relatively unchanging society their cross-cultural adaptations would be easier. But they are entering a society itself gripped with change. Not only are they having to learn in and about a new culture, but learn that culture in transition.

It is as difficult to make cross-cultural shifts in art as in any other area. The art children have learned may be based on cognitive styles, and perceptual experiences that we have never known. The ways they sort and organize visual information, the composition and design that has meaning to them, the symbols and visual qualities that give them pleasure may be strange to us (Coles and Scribner, 1976). Conversely, the art we expose them to, the things we encourage them to look at, the methods we use to stimulate them, and the cognitive styles we expect them to use in creating and responding to art are as foreign to those children as their ways are to us.

A given teacher may have almost as many cultures represented in a classroom as there are children. To try to make order out of this array teachers may stereotype children by race, by nationality or culture. This can leave the individual child or groups of children further alienated from school because they do not fit the teacher's stereotypes.

Finally, we need to ask, "How pervasive is cultural diversity?" Answers can come from state and local information, but often this is not thorough enough. The 1980 census still lumped people into Black, White, Hispanic, Asian, and others. This gives teachers little information about the many cultures and subcultures represented in these categories. Concerns are being raised that the 1990 census is not going to give us much more information

But they do indicate where concentrations of poverty exist even though many people are not counted. Poverty imposes some of its own pattern of culture and has continued unabated among the poor—whatever their racial and ethic origins. A report from the Urban Institute in Washington, D.C., by R. Minsky, shows a dramatic increase in the last 30 years of neighborhoods of impoverished people composed of mainly women heads of households and unemployed men (*Christian Science Monitor* 1/12/90, p. 8). In 1970 there were estimated to be 270 neighborhoods with a population of 752,000. By 1980 this had risen to 800 with 2,500,000 people. There are many indications that the 1990 census will show far more neighborhoods in this category, with many more people. This indicates increasing variation in culture as economic extremes increase.

For example, as large numbers of Afro-Americans have moved into much fuller participation in the overall society an inordinate number of others are living in these impoverished neighborhoods. This indicates increasing variation in Black culture and life style depending on where people live, their educational opportunities, achievements, and freedom from racism and sexism. These same differences can be found among many ethnic groups, and between sexes.

The tendency to lump all non-white peoples in composite figures by the numbers of minorities in a given city or state grossly masks cultural differences. But they do give us a better grasp of how our society is currently structured. *American Demographics* analyzed the percentages of minority children in our seven largest states. Texas, California, and Florida hover at 47%, New York at 40%, New Jersey at 37%, Illinois at 32%, and Michigan at 23% (May 1989). To have such high state averages usually means that in concentrated minority urban areas minorities are majorities!

In 1988 *The Department of Education, Center for Educational Statistics* gave reports on minority elementary and secondary school children in other states, the larger being those in the South and Southwest (Special Studies P-23 No. 159, pp. 36-39). Again, where the average is high the percentages in large cities or parts of cities go well beyond 50%. These figures do not separate recent arrivals, from those who have been here some time. We have not provided culturally relevant education for those children called minorities whose history in this country may go back before our establishment as a nation.

Geneva Gay, in the Banks book *Multicultural Education* (1989), reviews the experience of minority children who have access to unsegregated schools. As a whole they are placed in lower track classes. Such classes tend to stress memory and comprehension rather than thinking and making inferences. They are rewarded for being compliant and have less opportunity to interact with their teachers.

Many of these children are put into art classes but we have to ask ourselves if those classes are geared to their differing cultural ways of learning about and creating art. Are we giving them opportunities to extend, invent and make inferences if they so desire. Do they have as much time to interact with teachers as in higher tract classes?

What does this all mean? Foremost it means that we are a much more multicultural society than we have ever recognized; that we can no longer just teach from a middle class dominant culture perspective, but must have multicultural avenues for educating children. Perhaps we need to re-define what the over-all identity of this country is, what is in the pot that we are trying to melt and what are the implications for education.

In terms of art education we can begin by listening to students and observing their work as openly as possible to see what they are telling us of what has meaning in their cultural reality. What do they already know about art? What signs and symbols, what kinds of organization have significance? How do they like to learn? Later they can differentiate between the signs and symbols of corporate culture television, and the rich array of art subcultures that exist in this multicultural country, and then perceive them in the light of their own cultures' art.

We have been focusing on cultural differences in readiness to learn, and not how far or in what directions children can develop. They are all capable of becoming intercultural, of excelling and extending beyond the art of their own and other traditions. But they need a learning environment that respects and allows for cultural variety (McFee and Degge 1980). Those of us in teacher education and curriculum development may have to break out of middle class school art traditions to provide culturally relevant materials from which teachers can select and adapt for their students. Certainly the sociocultural foundations of art education need extensive development to create such curriculum and to help teachers use it.

Teaching the social and cultural meaning of art can help increase students cross-cultural sensitivity, respect for individual aesthetic roots and enable us to build a more cohesive multicultural society. It is hoped that such awareness will help us all be more compassionate with children who are learning in difficult multicultural situations. Comprehension of the cultural meaning of art can help us all find the wisdom we need during periods of pervasive culture change.

References

American Demographics, May 1989 quoted in *Christian Science Monitor* (January 2, 1990, p. 14).

Bourdieu, Pierre (1984) *Distinction: A social critique of the judgment of taste*. Cambridge, MA: Harvard University Press.

Cole, M. & Scribner, S. (1974) *Culture and Thought: A Psychological introduction*. New York: John Wiley, pp. 175-177.

Gay, Geneva (1989) "Ethnic minorities and educational equality," in J.A. Banks & C.A. McGee Banks (Eds.), *Multicultural education*. Boston: Allyn and Bacon, pp. 168-187.

McFee, J.K. & Degge R.M. (1980). *Art, Culture, and Environment*. Dubuque: Kendall Hunt. (Revised edition in press).

McFee, J.K. (1988). Cultural dimensions in the teaching of art, in F.H. Farley & R.M. Neperud (Eds.), *The foundations of aesthetics, art, and Art Education*. New York: Praeger, pp. 225-272.

McFee, J.K. (1995). "Change and the cultural dimensions of art education," in *Context, Content, and Community in Art Education: Beyond Postmodernism*. R.M. Neperud (Ed.). New York Teachers College Press, pp. 171-192.

Mincy, R. (January 12, 1990). Urban Institute Report, quoted in *Christian Science Monitor*, p. 8.

Schiller, H. R. (1989). *Culture inc.: The corporate takeover of public expression*. New York: Oxford University Press.

Snyder, T.D. (1988). *Digest of educational statistics*. National Center for Educational Statistics, U.S. Department of Education, p. 54.

5

DBAE AND CULTURAL DIVERSITY: SOME PERSPECTIVES FROM THE SOCIAL SCIENCES

DBAE Symposium, Austin, 1992

To introduce this paper, I will share my current perspective on the impact of our multicultural society on the content of art taught in schools, and on teaching-learning. Discipline Based Art Education (DBAE) has primarily used disciplines that contribute to the content of art education. I will posit that the socio-cultural, cognitive-perceptual, and learning areas of the social and behavioral science disciplines are needed also. They address differences in student aptitude to learn about, respond to, and create art. This paper will mainly address the socio-cultural disciplines needed in art education in a culturally diverse and changing society.

As I wrote this material, the Los Angeles explosion illustrated this country's gross ineptitude in accepting cultural diversity among its people and providing equal rights and opportunities. Trying to comprehend the complexities of this neglect leaves one almost speechless. Almost thirty years ago at the 1965 Penn State Seminar, some of us were calling for recognition of cultural diversity in art and among students. Equal opportunity to explore art as a basic mode of individual and social communication in one's own culture, as well as in others, was called for.

Now in 1992, the diversity is far greater. More people from most world cultures are here. The variation in background and language found in schools greatly compounds the dynamics of teaching-learning and the appropriateness of content.

Three other less obvious changes also exert strong influences on student readiness for learning. The divisive effects of poverty on the maintenance of culture is much more extensive than in 1965. Poverty diffuses the meaning of a given culture as experienced by children. In some parts of the country, particularly inner cities, the so-called dominant culture is no longer dominant, and the question of whose art to teach becomes paramount. The impact of changing mores and living styles is affecting most segments of the population and is affecting what children learn outside of school about who and what they are.

Art can no longer be considered for its own sake by everyone if that art is confined mainly within one cultural tradition. The cultural gulf between Western fine arts and a majority of our school population is greater than ever. This implies that the need for multicultural art being taught to children from many cultures and economic and social stratifications is essential. All students need to comprehend and critique art in their own culture to comprehend the meaning of art and culture in other people's lives. This will increase cross-cultural awareness and respect, insuring cohesion in our complex society. The visual arts are a pervasive part of the flow of information about individuals and groups, their identities, cherished meanings, and life styles. Misreading or ignoring the meaning in other people's art can lead to distrust and divisiveness, and reinforce prejudice, whereas awareness of others' culture and art can lead to acceptance of them as fellow human beings and can break up limiting stereotypes.

Some people are reacting to the Los Angeles, and increasingly national, crisis as proof that multicultural education has failed. The truth as I see it, watching from a long perspective, is that multicultural education has been too superficial. Exposing children to the art of a given culture without exploring the cultural context in which it was created and communicated, or without concern for the cultural diversity of the children taught, is a good example.

To clarify how I have arrived at these positions it may be useful to review the development of some of these ideas in my own thinking, and some of the areas students and I have worked on as we saw them developing within the art education literature.

A childhood experience exposed me to a profound idea. Early summer rains on Puget Sound confined us to our cabin. The only reading material was a collection of old magazines. In one, an anthropologist told of his first trip to a Pacific island. I could relate to that because we were on an inland sound of the Pacific Ocean and looked out on islands. He told of trying to communicate with an inquiring old woman whose one frame of reference for size, distance, proportion, and physical relationships was an island with a lagoon. He had to use this framework to answer her questions about where he came from and what it was like. Thinking about this as an adult, I realized that only in the degree he could break down his information into the units and qualities she could relate to was he even marginally able to help her grasp a world beyond her own. This example has helped me in trying to communicate with others with different cultures, frames of reference, cognitive maps, and styles.

My perspective on art education has also come from study in the arts, as a professional artist and as an art teacher. In the last role I became frustrated because too many students seemed remote from the subject I was so enthusiastic about. This led to study and teaching in the foundational areas of art and education. I selected parts of disciplines that addressed the socio-cultural, anthropological, psychological, and educational foundations of art education.

Many cultural anthropologists study art along with other aspects of culture. Some study art in different social classes of the same culture. They analyze such factors as art and belief systems, traditional and emerging symbols, concepts of what is art and the role of people who make it, their systems for making order, the historical pattern of acceptable artistic form, as well as differences between cultural groups in learning styles, responses to visual information, use of two- and three-dimensional space, what in the environment was selected to attend to, and the degree of creativity tolerated.

Cross-cultural psychologists place more emphasis on the study of individuals rather than the group, on how being a member of a cultural group directs the individual's development of cognitive style and perceptual mode as contrasted with individual development in other cultural groups. Continued interdisciplinary study needs to be made by art educators to keep the socio-cultural and behavioral foundations of art education up-to-date and usable for classroom practice and curriculum development.

From this interdisciplinary basis I have come to feel that one of the primary purposes of art education should be to teach art so it is culturally relevant to all our populations. Specifically this means enabling students from many cultural backgrounds to became aware of the ways art informs them of their own cultural values and patterns of living, and by studying other people's art to become open and knowledgeable of their culture. And they need to be allowed to learn using cognitive and perceptual styles they have already developed.

Learning art as cultural communication can become one of the basic language skills needed to participate in a multicultural democracy. Sensitive awareness of qualities and diversities in both art and culture can increase inter-cultural communication and respect, and can possibly reduce stereotyping and conflict. We have always struggled to keep art in the schools, but in this current crisis, when schools generally are bursting at the seams with diversity, we have to provide programs that meet the needs of children from diverse cultural backgrounds with differing cognitive and perceptual modes for apprehending and creating art.

We also have a responsibility to keep social interaction functioning by enabling students to comprehend and critique diversity of art in our midst. This need not detract from any one art form or art tradition but enable students to comprehend what a vital part art plays in defining who and what we are, and how we relate to each other. It is critical that they study other people's culture through the structure and nuances of their art as well as from what is spoken, written, and projected through journalistic television.

Our task, in developing curriculum and preparing teachers is to become aware of the cultural diversity that is found in our schools and to increase our knowledge of the ways art functions as communication of attitudes and beliefs in these different cultures. Such inquiry can help children respect their own background while becoming more sensitive to other's life patterns and art.

Teachers who use multicultural art education methods cannot be bound within one cultural system. They need to know of the cultures behind the arts they already know and both the art and the culture as they learn new ones. This helps them comprehend that children of very different cultures have attitudes, values, and art that are just as important to them as are those of the teacher.

With this attitude, both teachers and students can become aware of art as a window to culture. They may learn to see themselves as part of a culturally diverse society through the windows of many forms of art.

A second equally strong insight from the interdisciplinary work is that using teaching methods based on study of one single culture will not work in our current diversified schools.

The rest of my presentation will briefly review some of the history of the socio-cultural foundations of art education and some of the key concepts from the social sciences and art education theory that may be useful for you to consider.

History of the Socio-cultural Foundations of Art Education

I don't profess to having made a comprehensive study, but someone who was early and long involved, these are my recollections. Many important contributors are probably left out.

Questions about cultural and social class diversity were asked in the fifties and sixties concerning minorities. The folk arts of American Indians, Afro-Americans, Eskimos, Hispanics, and some Asians, in addition to earlier European immigrants, had been included in education for some time. It was hoped that by bringing these arts into the classroom all students would appreciate these contributors to American art. Some effort was made to help students accept minority people and their art as part of society. This direction was more internal to the United States and Canada than was the work of Ziegfeld in developing INSEA, to internationalize Art Education. As some of the same people were involved in both efforts, there was some overlap in interest.

In the mid-sixties, concern for the economically deprived children in our schools was discussed at the Penn State Seminar (Mattil, 1966). It was recognized that there were cultural differences among economically deprived students and that these evolved from the experience of being in poverty, as well as from cultural and ethnic origin.

During this period, the conflict of the counter-culture with the dominant culture arose over the right to question the established mores and culture patterns. This conflict spread throughout much of our society, among the working class, middle, professional, and upper classes in our schools and among artists and art educators. At the same time a resurgence of ethnic group history and art inquiry began.

Concern that Black art and culture was being ignored in mainstream education led some of the few Black art educators of the day, Gene Grigsby, James Smith, Howard Lewis, and Grace Hampton, to petition NAEA for a committee to address problems of minority teachers and students. In 1971 the NAEA Committee on Minority Concerns was formed. It is now a large group, includes other minorities, and is a regular part of NAEA conferences. Its members publish consistently. The anthology, *Art Culture and Ethnicity*, edited by Bernard Young, includes several members (Young, 1990). It includes case study and research of art among minority children, some studies of ethnic arts, and chronological review of journal articles on minority concerns.

The Women's Caucus was established in 1974 as part of NAEA. Members were part of the larger women's movement and were recognizing that there is a women's culture that is qualitatively different than men's culture of the same group, that women's art is influenced by this difference and is judged differently if the artist is known as a woman, that women are largely ignored in art history, and that girls in school are treated differently as art students than boys. There is an extensive body of literature by the Women's Caucus and considerable research by a fairly large number of people. Both of these groups' work needs to be analyzed and categorized for the socio-cultural foundations of art education. Their work led to changes in curricula and were some of the earlier forms of education for cultural diversity.

The INSEA conference on *Arts and Cultural Diversity* in 1978, in Adelaide, Australia, and most of their subsequent conferences dealt with the role of culture in affecting art forms and the implications for teaching in multicultural societies (Condous, 1980). The USSEA *Journal of Multicultural and Cross-cultural Art Education* established in 1982, the more recent AERA *Art and Learning*, and the NAEA *Journal of Social Theory Caucus* address theory, content and methods for teaching in culturally diverse settings. The Blandy and Congdon *Art in a Democracy* anthology addresses art education in a culture-, ethnic-, and class-diverse democracy (1987).

My own thinking about art multiculturally began in the mid-fifties, while studying with George Spindler, educational anthropologist, at Stanford. Also, I was much influenced by involvement in fieldwork with my anthropologist husband, Malcolm McFee. One of the most influential events was experiencing culture shock on returning from the Blackfeet Indian Reservation just east of the Rocky Mountains in Montana to our home in Palo Alto. It had been my first immersion in another culture, and, returning alone to my own cultural environment, my initial task was to pick up supplies at the local Sears store. Looking across that large abyss of goods and all that middle-class-Sears-store behavior put me in such culture shock I had to seek a wall to lean on.

Culture shock happens when you have become so involved in another culture that the act of returning to your home environment causes you to see your own background in stark reality, as you had never seen it before. People experience this in degree, but in some way it is needed by program developers and teachers to begin to realize how much of what they think and see as "reality" and as art is the result of learning a culture. People who have not experienced coming to grips with their own background can travel the world and not get out of that mind-set.

In my first book, *Preparation for Art*, published while teaching at Stanford (McFee, 1961), I focused both on the socio-cultural factors in learning about and producing art and on psychological studies of individual differences found in art behaviors. The content of art included international, folk, and environmental arts. But my doctoral students at Stanford mainly worked in the psychological area of perception.

It was only at Oregon in 1965, at the beginning of the counter-culture, that some dissertations dealt with multicultural concerns. I was writing the second edition of *Preparation for Art* with emphasis on the cultural dimensions (McFee, 1970). This was reflected in my teaching.

By 1975, Rogena Degge and I were writing *Art, Culture, and Environment,* trying to tie the dimensions of cultural diversity and individual differences in the perceptual, cognitive, and developmental, with classroom practice within the changing structure of American society (McFee, Degge, 1975, revised edition in press).

Since then, some former students from both the Stanford (1957-1962) and Oregon programs (from 1965 on) have been and are involved with the larger picture of art education in socio-cultural contexts. Efland in the social development of art; Silverman and Boyer in multicultural curricula; Chalmers and Lovano-Kerr in multicultural theory and practice; Degge in multicultural art education which includes environmental design and the cultural effects of television; Hamblen in interdisciplinary and cross-cultural theory and criticism of education practice; Congdon in Women's culture, folk, popular arts, and art education in democracy; Bev Jones in cross-cultural aesthetics, the impact of technology on art and art education and, most importantly, a methodology for interdisciplinary analysis; and Ettinger in an analysis of literature in multicultural art education and the effects of computergraphic design on communication. Nancy Johnson studied the subcultural values of docents in an art museum and the problems relating art education theories to multicultural teaching. Robyn Wasson did field work studying the art and life styles of Australian Aborigines in various stages of resistance to the dominant culture, and did critical studies of multicultural classrooms. Joanne Kurz Guilfoil studied Eskimo children's use of space and symbolism. At Stanford I was the only art educator working in this area at that time. At Oregon, students were influenced at differing times by Lanier, then Bev Jones and Rogena Degge who further developed the program after I retired in 1983.

Other art educators and their students each have a body of work that needs current review. Feldman and Ralph Smith, Francis Anderson, and Eisner and some of their students analyze cultural diversity from their particular theoretical positions, such as philosophy, curriculum, or art education as a discipline with its own methodology. The Wilsons have made critical studies of the implications for art for kids who learn their culture more from comics and

TV than any other source. Ecker, in recent years, has been doing important work with his international doctoral students who do fieldwork in their own countries and with some, like Michael Kendall with the Getty, who work here at home. Neperud and his students use cross-cultural-psychology and anthropology studies in cognition that show the effects of culture on how people see and experience art. Pat Stuhr at Ohio State, and Lynne Hart from McGill are two vigorous researchers in multicultural arts and education.

Chapman was and still is making significant observations with particular sensitivity to actual classrooms. Susan Mayer brings multicultural art education to the museum at the University of Texas. Eugene Grigsby, a master multicultural teacher, spent his classroom teaching and academic career helping students from very different backgrounds learn to respect themselves and their art. There are younger people extending this work even further. The main point is that there is an extensive body of work in our own literature that needs to be brought together with parts of the socio-cultural sciences for an interdisciplinary socio-cultural, teaching-learning foundation for DBAE.

My chapter on "Cultural Dimensions in the Teaching of Art" in the Farley, Neperud anthology, *The Foundations of Aesthetics, Art, and Art Education*, published in 1988, reviews literature related to multicultural education from anthropology, cross-cultural psychology, educational anthropology, and art education (Farley and Neperud, 1988).

A second chapter, "Change and the Cultural Dimensions of Art Education" in another Neperud anthology, *Context, Content, and Community in Art Education*, (Neperud, 1995), reviews literature on culture change and its effects on art teaching (Neperud). The following points about culture, cultural perspectives on art, and multicultural teaching are explored more fully in that chapter.

Development of the Concept "Culture"

The application of the word "culture" by anthropologists and cross-cultural psychologists differs from the more common use of the word which refers to a state of cultivated refinement in art and manners, which some people have and others do not. This generally refers to status within one culture. Anthropologists refer to the wide range of belief systems, patterns of behavior, and art which develop differently in some degree in each cultural group. Members of a cultural group share the patterns of behavior and belief system learned. By this definition, all groups of people have a culture and some forms of art within that culture. There will be variation among individuals in learning their culture, depending on how central or peripheral they are to the group.

Early field studies of remote people described their ideas, patterns of behavior, belief systems, status, and roles, including those of artists (Kluckhohn, 1951). Later studies looked at the ways of thinking which people in a given group learn (Geertz, 1984). These included studies of the differences in ways people learn to see, what that are taught to attend to. Some studied the ways people relate themselves to the group, from extreme group dependence, to strong independence. Differences in tolerance for change were also extensive.

Cross-cultural psychologists were concerned with variations in cognitive style, the ways people attend to, sort, and organize concepts, things, qualities, and quantities (Hofstede, 1984). Some have studied the way symbols take on significance, represent values, important events, changes in status, and objects of worship, and give reality to abstract ideas (Brislin, 1983). These symbols take on value of themselves, and people of one group value their own symbols and devalue the symbols of others. This is particularly important to understand in multicultural art education. Students may reject some arts, not because they cannot respond to the art, but because its symbolism comes from another group.

One study, done in France, has been made on cultural differences in social class, the attitudes toward art, and the use of visual forms to symbolize who and what people are and to enhance and give meaning to ritual (Bourdieu, 1984). Social class is rarely discussed in public discourse in an open society where it is assumed that all people have equal opportunity. But where social class, as it exists in practice, cultivates differences in values and attitudes, some attention needs to be paid to it in multicultural education. What is valued, what is attended to, how one thinks, how one values art can be significant points of misunderstanding.

Some anthropologists are trying to relate the concepts of culture to the increases in speed of mobility within cities and between regions, plus the acceleration of legal and illegal immigration, which leads to greater diversity of cultures in neighborhoods and schools as well as in regions of the country. We no longer have to go somewhere else to find carriers of other cultures; our neighborhoods may be microcosms of diversity (Clifford, 1987).

Culture Change

Whereas culture was originally thought of as a somewhat static state, it is now being seen as a system in which all parts are modified by other changes from inside and outside the group. Some parts may change, while others remain static. World interaction and modernization bring ideas, symbols, art, and values into groups that have been isolated for long periods. Television images and their environmental context raise questions about values. The almost instant imagery with which world events are seen affect the time sense in many societies. Sometimes these forces cause strong reactions and intense effort is exerted to reify traditional values.

People who move from one country to another will carry their cultural beliefs with less change if they settle into a group of their own people. Their ways of thinking, their values and beliefs will persist. Other people coming from the same place, carrying the same culture but settling in an unfamiliar setting may have more adjustments to make, and the culture pattern they carry may change the most.

Also people who are members of a cultural group may be at the core of the culture, while others move away from it. If too many people in a group are moving away from the core, this may change the culture of the whole. Subcultures may evolve for a time within a culture when the forces of culture change are too great.

Many children are growing up in multicultural families, with parents from different backgrounds. Sometimes the whole family will be living in a third cultural environment. Then we wonder why some of these children have a hard time relating to still a fourth culture—the American public school. Race or country of origin may give teachers few cues as to the culture or cultures a child is carrying, because of these factors of culture change that may be taking place. So when we talk about multicultural art education, we need to consider what states of culture change our students represent, as well as their background culture.

Art and Culture

I hesitate to say much about art and culture to this group, because you are all very expert in art and aesthetics. But there are some cultural aspects that come from anthropologists that may interest you. First is the problem that we all have to go beyond, our own culturally derived knowledge base, to try to observe the art of other cultures using their particular aesthetic. Often they do not have a system of formal aesthetics, but they do have culturally developed ideas of what is valuable about some of their art compared to others. It may have nothing to do with the art work itself, but who made it, or if the person who did it was of the right status, or how valuable it was. But I am reminded of museum docents I have heard in this country trying to impress school children by telling them how famous the artist is or economically valuable the work is and very little about the art itself and nothing about the cultural context from which it derived its meaning.

But culture does not always operate at the verbal level. A whole structure of ideas about what art is, what purposes it should serve, what emotional responses it evokes, how it should be used, and particularly how it should be created are so embedded in cultural learning that they are taken for granted. If we take our Western ideas of aesthetics for granted we will not recognize the screen we use to view other art. We will miss the communication of culture the art work represents. On the other hand, those who revel in the varied uses of visual qualities can derive much enjoyment from those qualities in the world's art and interpret the expressive qualities in terms of their own valuing system. But this also is a very limited view of what is there to be responded to.

You are well aware that our categories of fine, folk, and popular arts are not universals, even among all segments of our own society. We use concepts like primitive, or art from non-literate societies, in somewhat derogatory ways, yet same of these cultures may have complex oral histories and belief systems that are hardly primitive.

As with other aspects of culture, a given artist, or school of artists, may be trying to reify old values and slow down culture change. Some are moving with the current flow of the cultural system, while others are breaking out of the cultural mores and becoming cultural critics through art. They may be devising new ways of thinking, of depicting ideas, and of organizing messages. They may use qualities that are not culturally acceptable as art by some segments of the society. When people disagree, sometimes vindictively, it may mean that deep-seated and unanalyzed cultural values are being threatened. Other people who have struggled to break out of a cultural limitation may be most intolerant of artists who remain in the old pattern. We have to be careful in selecting art from other cultures because we could be choosing work that is peripheral to the culture. But if we do not show the range of art within a culture we can be giving a stereotyped impression.

There is a general consensus among those analyzing art forms in culture that art expresses values, reinforces concepts of reality, differentiates roles and status of people and things, provides the symbols that transmit meaning from one generation to another, increases the emotional involvement with rites of passage, transitions, and celebrations, illustrates the nuances and qualities of experience, and the concreteness, abstractness, and complexity of thought, and is a record upon which the members of a

73

culture can reflect on the meaning of their particular identity as a group of people (Silver, 1979).

There is also some agreement that the full range of visual arts impact upon people, and that in public schools the arts that are represented by the students' cultures should be considered. This means that fine arts, crafts, folk arts, advertising and graphics, costume and environmental arts, cartoons and comics, popular arts and television be investigated. Though some cultures may not have all categories, a fuller range of all their arts could be included.

Multicultural art criticism needs extensive development. My thinking at present is that as we develop inter-cultural awareness of art we will find clusters of criteria to evaluate the ways art sustains, transmits, and reacts to cultural structures and practices. Art may be judged not only for what it says but how well it says it within its cultural context. Then we will have a core of evaluation for multicultural art criticism. This does not diminish the worth of evaluating any one culture's art in terms of its own aesthetic and modes of criticism if people recognize this as operating within a cultural system.

In this paper, I can barely touch on the literature on "art and culture" but refer you to my review of work by Bourdieu, Silver, Geertz, Clifford, and the controversial Maquet (McFee, in Neperud, in press), as well as the literature by cultural theorists who include the functions of art as manifestations of culture.

Implications for Culturally Diverse Art Education

A multicultural *setting* occurs when a teacher from one cultural background and art tries to teach children from another culture. It could be an American-born, middle-class Mexican-American teaching immigrant Mexican children from different cultures in Mexico. It could be an upper-middle-class teacher with a broad background in fine arts trying to teach children whose exposure to art has been the visual forms and design in television and mass production. It happens when thousands of teachers try to reach children who have come to this country carrying other cultures, or who live in conclaves of people from their family's culture. Wherever the teacher's background culture differs from those of at least some of the students, a multicultural setting exists.

But multicultural art *teaching* takes place only if the teacher comprehends the functions of art in cultures and the background and art of the students. Here and in most other urban centers, the same teachers may have as many cultures represented in the classroom as they have students. The range of diversity in classes requires that we develop strategies for teaching art in multicultural settings, even though a single teacher cannot understand all the diversity represented.

In this brief look at a very complex teaching situation, some kinds of inquiry strategies seem workable. As stated at the beginning, the emphasis can be on studying art as cultural communication. This requires ability to relate what is said through art to its cultural context, such as analyzing an art to find clues to the artist's culture. Then students can compare the art to descriptions of the culture to discover how well they have interpreted the art. Examples of different arts and different descriptions of culture can be analyzed to discover which art fits with which group and why. Through asking students what messages they get from the art, how it is organized, how it is made, and how they think the people valued it, they have a basis for looking at the different cultural descriptions to find the strongest relationships.

In some cases curriculum developers can use culture-based social studies programs in elementary schools and middle schools to relate art inquiry to the peoples being studied to see how much can be learned through art about the essence and quality of their lives. Then students can learn how the values and attitudes of those people affect the way the art is created compared to the art and culture of other groups. Then reflection can begin on how we use art in our cultures to express who and what we are. Inquiry can be made about the differences between the many kinds of art we have in our society and their kinds of messages, to whom they are directed, and for what purposes.

In schools where the background cultures are varied, teachers need skills in inquiry to see what children select among varied art forms and why they like and dislike them. Children's own paintings may give clues about how they organize, what is important for them to depict, and how much they are being influenced by new cultural factors such as television.

The sequencing of these types of inquiry will depend on the particular class. Each inquiry area can be developed at different aptitude levels. It would be possible to develop programs where children proceed at their own pace or select the cultures or art where they wish to begin their inquiry.

The preparation of teachers for culturally diverse settings requires that they study cultures and the functions of art in them. Some experience should be provided that helps them comprehend how much they are bound within their own cultural systems—in the ways they think and see, in the ways they organize their significant world, in their likes and dislikes about art. Courses for teachers in the cultural history of world art are needed.

Studio work where the different backgrounds of students are given consideration would surely help. Art education courses should integrate coursework into a theoretical and practical framework which will help teachers learn to use new culturally diverse curricula and resource material, develop teaching materials for their particular setting, and increase their individual sensitivity and confidence in teaching in a culturally diverse society. This can help heal the explosive conflicts that arise from inter-cultural misunderstanding.

References

Blandy, D. and Congdon, K.G. (Eds.) (1987). *Art in a Democracy*. New York: Teachers College Press.

Bourdieu, Pierre (1984). *Distinction: A Social Critique of the Judgment of Taste*. Cambridge, MA: Harvard University Press.

Brislin, R.W. (1983). "Cross cultural research in psychology," *Annual Review of Psychology, 34* (363-400).

Clifford, James (1988). *The Predicament of Culture*. Cambridge, MA: Harvard University Press.

Condous, Jack (1980). *Arts in Cultural Diversity*. INSEA 23rd World Congress, Adelaide-Sydney: Holt, Rinehart and Winston.

Geertz, C. (1983). *Local Knowledge*. New York: Basic Books.

Hofstede, G. (1984). "Cultural consequences: International differences in work-related values," *Cross-cultural Research and Methodology Series, Vol. 5*. Beverly Hills, CA: Sage Publications.

Kluckhohn, C. (1951). "The study of culture." In D. Lerner and H. D. Lasswell (Eds.), *The Policy Sciences*. Stanford, CA: Stanford University Press, 86.

Maquet, Jacques (1986). *The Aesthetic Experience: An Anthropologist Looks at the Visual Arts*. New Haven, CT: Yale University Press.

Mattil, Edward L. (Ed.) (1966). *A Seminar in Art Education for Research and Curriculum Development*. University Park: The Pennsylvania State University Press.

McFee, J. K. (1961). *Preparation for Art*. Belmont, CA: Wadsworth Publishing Co.

McFee, J. K. (1970). *Preparation for Art*, Second Edition. Belmont, CA: Wadsworth Publishing Co.

McFee, J. K. and Degge, R. (1977). *Art, Culture, and Environment*. Belmont, CA: Wadsworth Publishing Co. Paperback edition (1980) Dubuque, IA: Kendall Hunt Publishing Co. (Revised edition in press, 1998).

McFee, J. K. (1988). "Cultural dimensions in the teaching of art." In *The Foundations of Aesthetics, Art, and Art Education*. F.M. Farley and R.W. Neperud (Eds.). New York: Praeger.

McFee, J. K. (1995). "Change and the cultural dimensions of art." In Neperud, R.W. (Ed.) *Context, Content, and Community in Art Education: Beyond Post Modernism.*

Silver, H. R. (1979). "Ethno art," *Annual Review of Anthropology,* 8:267-307.

Young, Bernard (1990). *Art, Culture, and Ethnicity.* Reston, VA: The National Art Education Association.

Reprinted with permission. From "DBAE and Cultural Diversity: Some Perspectives from the Social Sciences." Getty Center for Education in the Arts Seminar on Discipline Based Art Education and Cultural Diversity, Austin, Texas, 1992.

6

INTERDISCIPLINARY AND INTER-NATIONAL TRENDS IN MULTI-CUL-TURAL ART EDUCATION

National Taipei Teachers College, 1995

Introduction

This paper is based on five assumptions: 1) that everyone's culture has some form of visual art; 2) that art is a major form of communicating who and what a people are; 3) that the world is getting so small that almost everyone needs to learn to relate to other cultures; 4) that a majority of schools world-wide are in some degree multi-cultural; and 5) that only when the teacher's and student's cultures are the same and they live in cultural isolation should a single culture's art be taught. For all these reasons, the teaching of art needs to be, in large degree, multi-cultural.

The subject art and the subject culture are so interwoven that I will deal with them in relation to each other throughout this paper. You cannot discuss art and then add culture. Art and culture interact at almost every point from the cultural system which nurtured the artist to the impact its message has within its own and other cultures. We will deal with these in the context of education.

The format of this paper begins with world trends that affect all education today, then I will identify those experiences that led me to contribute to the field of multi-cultural and cross-cultural visual art education. Following definitions and descriptions of the concepts culture and art, I will then describe the interdisciplinary structure of the field and its academic foundations. The last part of the paper is an analysis of some of the effects of cultural training on children's responses to art, using research from the social and behavioral science foundations of art education.

World Trends

Before getting into the heart of this paper, let me make some observations about world trends that affect our view of multi-cultural art and education today. On one hand, access to information through the international computer internet, electronic mail, world wide fax machines and almost instant radio and television are shrinking our time while exploding our access to the vast mental world of images and ideas. On the other hand, there are increasing numbers of smaller cultural groups, each with its own somewhat different pattern of values, concepts of reality, and social order vying with each other for control of territory, ethnicity, and government. Each is reasserting its identity and independence from other groups. What were once national cultures, with sub-cultures within an overall framework of values are in some cases breaking up to save the sub-culture's identity, values, and the art that expresses them.

Montreal, for example, is a city that is part of the French-speaking, French-culture area of Canada. In order to separate itself politically, socially, linguistically, and visually from English-speaking Canada, it is tearing down British buildings and city symbols and reinforcing those that are historically French as they continue to build a modern international city.

These two powerful forces, a common worldwide information pool and a deep desire to preserve separate cultural identities, are at work at different levels of world consciousness. One force is moving towards worldwide access to information and ideas and the other towards greater cultural independence. I cannot claim to understand the impact of these two on each other, but in many parts of the world people are in conflict over whose cultural values will have the highest political power—yet any one of them with the internet can turn a switch and be on a worldwide communication system with myriad cultural ideas and images.

Why is all this important to us as educators? Because all the cultures use art and visual imagery to identify who they are. But they will bomb and destroy other cultures, people, cities, art, and architecture to preserve their own ideas and images. This leads me to believe that multi-cultural art and architecture understood through diverse cultural aesthetics, cultural images, design and ranges of creativity can help humanize our understandings of each other across cultural lines. Through art we can comprehend and thus learn to respect each other's culture and through awareness of other's culture be able to appreciate each other's art. This is a reciprocal process.

About 20 years ago my husband and I spent two months living in the Chinese YMCA in Singapore. Every late afternoon we observed local children watching television programs of stereotyped American situational comedy of an idealized middle class American family. We were impressed that the stereotypes produced in the film were far from realities and were only a simplistic idealized view of family life, its values and the visual symbols used to support it. Certainly it was only a very modest form of theater art. But this illustrates a critical question of multi-cultural art education. How can we make the interface of art and culture provide genuine understanding between art and its cultural context and children's culturally learned ways of responding to art. As we watched the children, we could only wonder what was going on in their thinking based on their own cultural experience. By their expressions and responses they were seeing things differently than we were. They saw humor when we did not. What was supposed to be humorous to us was not to them.

To make art the avenue for cross-cultural understanding, so needed in the world today, we are impelled to address differences in meanings whether between sub-cultures or transmitted through the internet.

Perspectives on History of MC and CCAE

I have been asked to give you some of the history of my work in this area. You must remember that in some large degree I am a captive of my own culture. But through the years certain key experiences have helped me gain a broader view. Briefly let me share with you some of these events so you can better interpret my ideas. I grew up in Seattle, a northwest port city of the United States to Asia and Alaska. We were at the end of a long push westward and our horizons were still in that direction. Our main art museum was predominantly of Asian art which was broadly represented in affluent people's homes. Northwest coast Indian and Eskimo art had a strong influence. We were exposed to arts of the Pacific, but learned little of the cultures they represented. In the mid-thirties when I first started exhibiting as a painter, the effects of these cultures' art and the misty forested and inland sea environment was converging with my exposure to the expressionist and cubist art movements of the times. I studied with Alexander Archipenko, the great Ukrainian sculptor, who on observing my first still life, told me never to paint like that again—and I didn't. I had been following a cultural pattern of what was considered to be acceptable art and this kind, gentle but powerful artist helped me go beyond it. I must say more with ideas than with paint. The next important event was going to Stanford to get a doctorate in Education. Here the study of cultural anthropology helped me understand much of my prior experience. Not much work on anthropology and art was developed then, but there was much an artist-teacher could derive from this study to see the relationships. Also my husband, a philosophy major, intrigued by what I was studying, changed majors and ultimately became a cultural anthropologist. I shared some of Malcolm McFee's field work with American Blackfeet Indians.

A key experience was teaching in Arizona, where students with Master's of Western Fine Arts degrees were having trouble teaching American Indians, African Americans, Hispanics, and urban poor of all races. It was an opportunity to search cultures and arts to find ways to make the study of other peoples art more meaningful to all students.

My years at the University of Oregon began in 1965 during the counter-culture revolution where the dominant culture values were challenged by young people. Doctoral students came from Asia and Middle Eastern countries, and from Australia, Canada and New Zealand. The main focus of doctoral study was cross-cultural.

During the late sixties and seventies I taught art education during summer school in Hawaii. My students were school teachers, predominantly of Asian descent, and were carriers of their background cultures as well as being Americans.

Recently I worked with classroom teachers in Los Angeles County who were working on Master's Degrees in Art Education. It is estimated that 120 different languages are spoken by elementary school children in that county. This means that as many different culture patterns, values, arts, attitudes and ways of learning are also there. This has forced me to look on multi-cultural art education from a worldwide view as little of the world is not represented in Los Angeles schools today.

The focus of my writing beginning with my dissertation back in 1957 and first book *Preparation for Art* in 1961 was on psychological and cultural differences among children (McFee, 1961, 1967, 1970). Through the years, doing invited research papers for conferences and chapters for anthologies and subsequent books (McFee, 1977, 1980, 1992) helped me focus more on the cultural factors and showed the changing social context.

The Pennsylvania State Seminar in Art Education (1965) identified its foundational fields as psychology, anthropology, sociology, aesthetics, art history, studio arts and curriculum.

I spent a year researching and writing a paper for that conference on socio-economic and cultural factors in children's aptitudes for art. The melting pot idea was still in vogue and we were mainly concerned with the poor and a few minority groups, mainly African-Americans and Hispanics.

In 1978 I prepared a review of research in the social sciences for the INSEA (International Society for Education Through Art) in Adelaide, Australia. Its purpose was to help us understand the functions of art in culture and society, as well as cultural diversity. INSEA continues to be the major worldwide organization of art educators—and usually stresses the multi-cultural and cross-cultural aspects of the field. (1978)

Between that conference and the next one in 1986 for a joint Canadian and U.S. Societies for Education in Art conference, the impact of the second largest wave of immigration of peoples from all over the world was changing both countries and multi-cultural art was getting much more attention. (1986)

There are two anthologies where I have written extensive reviews of research on this topic, one edited by Farley and Neperud in (1988) and the second edited by Neperud now being produced by Teachers College Press at Columbia University. The latter includes reviews of the growing work by art educators using anthropology and sociology as a base (1995).

I have just finished a monograph for the National Art Education Association in the U.S. bringing together my papers on cultural diversity in art and among students from 1965 to 1995. By analyzing the problems addressed over those years, trends are found towards increasing cultural diversity among students and a growing recognition of the presence of more cultures' art (McFee, In press)

Definition and Descriptions of Culture and Art

Now I need to clarify my use of the concept culture and of art. The culture pattern of a group of people includes their learned and shared values, their concepts of reality and belief systems, their structure of social roles and acceptable behaviors, their expectations of how others will or should behave, and how cohesive is the power of the group on the individual. It includes their rituals, symbols of communication, their art and patterns of design and habitat. It also impacts the way they learn to see, to think and to organize their reality. It includes how the self is seen in relation to the group.

The most central and perhaps most difficult question for all of us to learn is that we, ourselves, are culture bound—that is, we have learned to see, think, value, organize, and behave in large part from the cultural backgrounds we have had. These taken for granted ways of thinking and valuing underlie our responses to art. They also affect how we teach and evaluate others' art.

For most of us, it takes deep involvement in a culture different from our own to force us to come back and see our own art and culture objectively. This intense experience is called "culture shock." It happens most often when we return to our own after being immersed in another culture. We see what is familiar more objectively; it is less taken for granted.

But we can move across continents or around the world carrying our cultural balloon so tightly around us that we only see others and their art from our perspective, never theirs—see their art by our ways of seeing and valuing and not see it from theirs. We experience no culture shock on returning. We may be a teacher of art in a multi-cultural classroom and only see our students as different from us, but rarely as valued individuals who see themselves and art through their own cultural perspectives.

One experience of culture shock helps us see the reality of the effects of culture, but it takes many long looks at our own background and involvement in other cultures to be aware of our own cultural embeddedness.

The first time I experienced culture shock was in a large department store on a busy Saturday morning in California. I had just returned from three months with my husband who was deeply involved studying the Blackfeet Indians. He was studying their sense of reality, values, expectations, their sense of self and others, and their hunting and gathering behaviors as adapted to the sparse environment of rural Montana, a state in the northwest of the United States.

Both cultures stood out in such stark reality because they were significantly different. The surroundings in which the two groups of people had "learned to be" were so disparate one could not move easily from one to the other. Nor could I return to aspects of my own culture and see it as previously taken for granted. This was partly because I had so identified emotionally and intellectually with the Indians that seeing part of my own familiar environment again produced a strong reaction—even physically. I was in such a state of shock I had to find a wall to lean against.

Ideally we should be so aware of cultural diversity that we are not threatened by it, but have a rich reservoir of cross-cultural experiences among different people and different visual arts. Then we can help each child explore the world of art from their own perspective, even as they become more aware of other people's art and culture. But it is most important to realize that many school children are facing culture shock as they move from familiar settings to environments where the cultural values and the ideas, actions, and images that express them are so different.

Visual Art

At the present time definitions of visual art and aesthetic order vary widely in the world. Some cultures have no such concept as art or aesthetics in their language yet have objects that we would call art and concepts of what has aesthetic value and what does not. The range of objects that are included as part of art are still varied. Some cultures include a wide range of activities and objects to describe the results of art activity, others do not.

I have used the following definition of art for some time. Here is a current variation: Art is the result of that form of human behavior by which people purposefully interpret and enhance the quality or essence of experience through the things produced. It ranges from the simplest enhancement of a tool to the expression of the most profound projections of individual and group experience in designed visual form. It varies from simplest artifact to the plan of cities, from personal expression to the summation of a dynasty. It includes some of the moving images transmitted by film, television, and beginning now on the internet.

We can study art to see what cultural values, belief systems, sense of reality, organization of space, symbols, and aesthetic preferences, as modified over time, are expressed in a people's art. We can look for cultural confluence—when art of one culture is influenced by the art or values of another culture. Both the visual qualities and the content message are influenced by culture and cultural confluence. As culture changes so does art. Studying art as cultural communication can bring it into a more central position in children's learning and they can recognize its vast impact on themselves and their own communities as well as opening bridges to other people's art and culture.

We can help children learn to see and use more of the functions of art. It is used to enhance ceremony and ritual. It makes subjective values, attitudes and beliefs have more objective reality. It is a mode of analysis, of recording and transmitting information from one generation to another—thus providing cultural continuity. It heralds and sometimes innovates change. It also separates and categorizes events, status of people and activities, defines roles and gives the role bearer a sense of stability in his or her place. It expresses the systems of organization, of time and space of a people. It is an avenue of celebration, of criticism, of transcendence, of despair. It is full of culture and a very fundamental mode of communication.

85

Foundational Fields of Multi-Cultural Art Education

Now I will give you my interpretation of this field's foundations, those areas of study that can contribute to the practice of our field. Some of them are quite highly developed, others much less so. Some have been developed in only one or two cultures. All need a much broader cultural base.

The *first* foundation is a culturally based art history. This includes the study of the cultural roots and culture changes over time of a people's art. It includes the study of the effects of cultural confluence—the influence of other cultures on the historical development of an art form. Traditionally, Western Art History has been the history of the art and artist and less of the cultural context in which the artist was nurtured and the art created. Comparative aesthetics in different cultures needs much more development analyzing the ways concepts of beauty are developed and as art is judged as having quality and form as in art criticism.

The history of Asian and Western Fine Arts is well studied, but their cultural history has been less developed. Also the broad base of arts, crafts, computer graphics, film, television, and popular arts, has only recently been included. A cross-cultural anthropology of art would compare the ways art is used to express values, attitudes, beliefs, social structure, as well as culturally based aesthetics. There is actually a great need for a new interdisciplinary foundation that includes culture-based art history, aesthetics and art criticism with the anthropology of art into a synthesis from which multi-cultural visual arts can be studied.

The *second* foundation is the psycho-cultural. This includes multi-cultural study of perception, cognition, learning, and creativity. Considerable progress has been made in the field of educational anthropology and some art educators have used this work as a take-off point. They are all concerned with the ways living in a culture affects individual development and thus to responses to different kinds of art. As in the first foundation new developments are needed relating psychological factors which have been studied in only a few cultures, to include more of the cultural factors which can affect behavior.

The *third* foundational area is in education itself. For our purposes its theories of learning, curriculum development, teaching strategies, evaluation all have to be adapted to cultural differences among children and their aptitudes to respond to the arts from different cultures.

The terms multi-cultural and cross-cultural also need defining as I am using them here. There are multi-cultural classrooms because many cultures are represented among the students. There are multi-cultural children who carry in themselves more than one culture. There are multi-cultural arts where more than one culture's forms and symbols are manifested in one object of art. There are multi-cultural arts when more than one culture's art is represented together. Cross-cultural experience takes place when a viewer of one culture observes the art of another culture. There is crosscultural experience when teacher and learner must cross cultures to teach or learn from the other. The success of the experience depends on how much crossing takes place.

Much cross-cultural activity takes place within multi-cultural teaching situations. Most every child-art-teacher relationship is somewhat different cross-culturally because the children, the art and the teacher may represent varied cultures. Thus, somewhat different cross-cultural connections need to be made, even within one classroom. The ways parents and boys or girls have learned their own culture also creates multi-cultural situations.

Cultural Diversity in Art Responses

Now after presenting a broad picture of multi-cultural and cross-cultural Visual Arts education, I will take one aspect of this larger framework and relate research on the affects of culture on some of children's modes of responding to art.

Art teachers in complex multi-cultural classrooms cannot know all they need to know about the cultures represented by their students, but they can be helped by identifying points where students may be different in their responses.

Some cultural anthropologists and cross-cultural psychologists, along with art educators, have identified these points. Detailed reporting of this research can be found in my chapters in the Farley and Neperud (1988) and Neperud anthologies (1995).

The points where children's culturally learned abilities may lead to differences in their responses to art are as follows: 1) their familiar and preferred images, symbols and design qualities; 2) their culturally learned perception, cognition, and systems of ordering; 3) their group or selfcentered motivations; 4) their socio-cultural stratification and its art; and 5) their exposure to culture change.

Familiar Images, Symbols, and Design Qualities

Students from different cultures have varying reservoirs of remembered images and symbols that have meaning to them and that are preferred by them. They have generally learned to favor familiar design qualities such as kinds of texture, color, line, use of space, shape and size, as found in their visual background. They have also learned acceptable ways of organizing and designing these elements. There are wide variants; traditions of design, structure, function. Each is based on the members of the culture's ways of seeing and organizing visual information, as well as their values.

When children reject or are unmotivated by symbols that are not familiar, it doesn't mean they lack a capacity to respond to images and symbols. It may only mean the ways these images are created are too foreign and the quality strange. The way they are designed may not be as ordered or varied as they have learned to like them.

It is not only that children learn different symbols and the ways these are designed, but they use these as modes of thinking, of trying to understand what is going on. Young children's drawings illustrate in some degree how they construct and organize what they have learned from their experience visually, emotionally and symbolically.

Brislen, a cross-cultural psychologist, has studied the functions of symbols in culture (Brislen, 1983, pp. 363-400). He finds they are used to express the values of the members of that culture, but they take on a meaning of their own. The symbol itself, not what it stands for alone has value as a cultural artifact. We prefer the symbols of our culture more than the symbols of other cultures. We see and attend to the familiar more than the strange.

This sheds light on the symbol creation of adolescents who are establishing for themselves a visual system that sets them and their peers apart from the previous generation, or other adolescent groups. The graffiti urge is, in part, to make their statement of values clearly seen by others. They think they have to do this to establish their identity and status. A war of symbols sometimes goes on as cities paint over adolescents' art to keep their own familiar symbols of places and streets undisturbed. The symbols take on a reality of their own. When one's symbols are defaced or destroyed, one tends to react more strongly to protect or project them.

But the effect of symbols and visual qualities on people begins with small children. Before learning to read they have learned to respond to their environment in terms of what is visually present. I once had in tow a noisy four year old who was attempting to climb up, over or under everything along a busy street. I had to turn into an exclusive, carpeted jewelry store to pick up a watch repair. Once in the door, the child's behavior radically changed. He was quiet and subdued. I had said nothing but he apparently read the qualities of the place as symbols and changed his behavior. But he was much relieved to get back to the street and immediately resumed his former behavior.

88

Culturally Learned Perception, Cognition, and Ordering

Now we will look at the ways growing up in a cultural group affects the ways a child perceives, structures its thinking and orders its ideas and images.

I did a descriptive study of fourth grade children in middle and lower income neighborhood schools in six American cities (McFee, 1971). One task was to draw a picture of their city. More children from middle income families drew networks of freeways. This was the strong image and pattern they had learned from experience of how the city was held together. It was a way of organizing reality, and a means of thinking about the city. Children's drawings from lower income [families] were more street oriented. Apparently they had less freeway experience. Their reality was their more congested neighborhood street and its activity. Cultural patterns of behavior can vary between economic groups in the degree that they limit or extend experience.

But the differences can be deeper. Some years ago, before television exposure, children of two different cultures in Saipan were given Rorschach Tests by psychologists Joseph and Murray to see if they responded to fine or large detail (Joseph and Murray, 1957). They ranged in age from 5 to 17 with 50 boys and 50 girls in each group. The Carolinian children made twice as many large detail responses and saw images as whole things, while Chamorro children looked for fine detail and created images from them. Their culturally learned patterns for seeing apparently had taught them to look for certain kinds of images and feel free to respond to them but to give less attention to others.

If a teacher's motivating tasks and examples of art are one or the other, they will not be motivating some of the students. In the United States there was once a motivating technique used by art teachers. They encouraged students to "Work big and fill the page," but their fine-detail oriented students had a problem—a cultural problem—because that is not their learned pattern for seeing, looking, and organizing their world. Many teachers found this did not work with the large number of Vietnamese children who were coming to their schools. They preferred fine-detailed art to observe, and worked patiently on their own careful, intricate effort.

For some people it is very difficult to accept that others see or structure their thinking differently than they do. When others design and organize in unfamiliar ways, they are often categorized as not very "artistic." What is artistic for these people is actually a culturally derived concept—not necessarily a universal one, or applicable in many other cultures. A large body of research in perceptual and cognitive psychology has been used for some time by cross-cultural psychologists to show that the ways people have learned to see affects what they attend to, how they sort and organize it (Berry, 1980).

Group or Self-Centered Motivation

The ways individuals from different cultures relate to others has a strong influence on how they are motivated. It affects whom they turn to for approval, what they attend to, their choices, and what they create as art.

In some cultures art teachers stress individual creation, self-directed innovation, expressing the self and self evaluation. Yet more of the world's children come from societies where one finds oneself more in the group, are motivated by it and are accepted or rejected by group norms. Their culturally learned sense of self is not so differentiated from others. Children most motivated by their group are less inclined to turn inwardly for motivation to achieve. They would respond to art or create art in terms of what was acceptable to their own cultural aesthetic norms.

A very important study of the goals for preschools in Japan, mainland China, and Hawaii was done by Tobin, Wu, and Davidson. It illustrates how the needs of society are translated into educational goals that affect how children see themselves in relation to the group (1989).

In mainland China, where the birth rate is limited to one child per family, some preschools compensate for the overprotection and indulgence of four grandparents and two parents on the developing sense of self of one child. In preschool they are taught to work in groups, in quiet, orderly ways and at specific times and places. Teachers expect them to be self-reliant within a disciplined group.

The historic Japanese cohesive extended families are more separated now and most children grow up in smaller immediate family groups. So preschools foster socialization and getting along in larger groups, Teachers supervise more remotely and let children solve their interpersonal problems.

They are allowed to be spontaneous, playful, and argumentative and to use space freely.

In the preschools in Hawaii a majority of children come from both parents or single parent working families. So teachers fill the gap of a need for more personal attention. Their relations with children are more tactile and immediate. Children are picked up and comforted to help them have more assurance of their self-worth. They have more freedom of choice within the activities. But the stronger socialization skills of Japan and group belonging skills in mainland China are not stressed.

Each of these groups of children have already had two different cultural behavior patterns taught them: those of the home and the preschool. They may not have given up their family values for preschool values. They are learning a new relationship between the self and the group in each of these three cultures. They may turn to the family or the preschool patterns for motivation and approval.

All these factors would suggest that children's own art work can help us by seeing what cultural factors are influencing them, by the symbols they use, by the traditions expressed, their sense of organization and use of detail.

An interesting study by Hofstede, a cross-cultural psychologist, looked for differences in individual versus group orientations among different cultures within the western tradition (Hofstede, 1984). He found that people are motivated by how they see themselves and behave in relation to the group as a result of their culturally learned way of achieving.

Hofstede also found that in Spain, Portugal, Yugoslavia, and France there is a strong need for security and group solidarity. In Greece and in German speaking societies, it is for individual security. In Great Britain, their dominions and former colonies such as Canada and the United States, the most powerful force for motivation is in personal, individual success.

Among the northern European countries, including the Netherlands, it is for collective success of belonging and the living environment. The same art study would be seen and critiqued in different ways by children from these nationalities. Some would want it to conform to their group norms, others would not accept art that threatened their security, while still others would question its importance to their success.

Clifford Geertz, an anthropologist, makes some broad observations about cultural differences in the relationships of individuals to their physical and social environment between overall western and other cultures. According to his study people in western cultures see the individual as separate from nature, a center of "awareness, emotion, judgment and action"—a unique being (Geertz, 1983). Other cultures often see less separation of the individual from nature or the individual from the group and assume more likeness between individuals.

These differences would affect the aesthetics of a group, the basis on which they can learn, their ways of seeing, attending and organizing and their preferred meaningful symbols.

One caution here, even though a study like this may show a tendency toward one pattern of values or another, it does not mean that all people in a culture will be the same. Some are moving out, some are adhering to the center.

In some cultures producing art is considered to be an individual thing. In others it is learning a very culturally prescribed form of art. Children who have learned to be self expressive may have trouble responding to disciplined art—and those who have learned to discipline their work have trouble relating to less structured art. In other words, children who were rewarded by being like the group—following the tradition—will probably like art that is motivated by the cultural group. Whereas children whose cultural art forms are very diverse may prefer arts from other cultures that reward diversity.

Teachers need to be very alert that some children need or expect more personal encouragement and reward from the teacher, others get their rewards from the group and still others more from themselves, such as through opportunities to compare their own work over time. But some children, confused by culture shocks, may need more adjustment time and tolerance as they try to find a way to cope with school and themselves in the new situation. Having familiar art to respond to may be necessary until they feel more adapted to their new situation.

Socio-Cultural Stratification and Its Art

A nation, or culture, may be stratified by social class, by traditional roles or by economics or both. Art is often stratified as well. Membership in a status or class can affect what children have learned to prefer.

French anthropologist, Pierre Bourdieu, studied the varied art symbols that people in different social and economic classes use in France (Bourdieu, 1984). He shows how, in a complex cultural society, sub-cultures have developed around different social and economic classes. Each class has symbols, art, artifacts, and environments that clearly identifies its social standing in the overall culture of France. In this way, these selections by these groups give a hierarchy of values to art, and the art signifies hierarchies of social stratification of people.

The art and symbols of each group clearly express group identity and this provides individuals and families with a sense of belonging. It reinforces the culturally defined relation of the self to their group. This indicates that in a given classroom, children may have quite different kinds of art and design they relate to because of their social class. When a child's art preferences are rejected by the teacher, the child may take this as a rejection of his most meaningful group and his or her self in relation to it.

Each economic hierarchy represents a sub-cultural value system. Sub-cultures appear to grow up around art forms. The different folk arts, women's art, and popular arts have groups of people who value and support them, as do all the fine arts and crafts. The artist's identity is related to the group that supports it.

For years I taught a graduate seminar on Art and Society. We studied the ways art forms were used to communicate who a particular group was and what their values were. Students explored many types of social groups to see how they identified themselves through art. Some were not usually considered as being art forms because of their so-called lower social status.

A young woman who had never thought of going to a wrestling match was taken to one. She was fascinated by how the costuming and dancing of the performers was contrasted between "good guys" and "bad guys." She documented with film how a "bad guy" was transformed into a "good guy" by slowly, over time, changing his costume and his movements. In other words, costume and kind of movement identified the cultural meaning of good and bad.

Another student analyzed the art work decorating a national women's motorcyclist club "bikes." While they wore mechanics overalls, their bikes were very feminine, gaudily floral and predominantly pink. It would appear that their personal clothing gave them status in the world of skilled riders, but their bikes showed their stereotype of their other culture—being female.

These examples may seem extreme, but they show how groups with different socio-economic status symbolize their standing. They also illustrate the variety of visual environments in which students may have grown up. They show that visual symbols are used not only to express values, attitudes and belief systems, but identify status and class as well. Everyone uses them in some degree to express their identity, differentiate it from others, and enhance their group belonging and individual role.

Cultural Change

There is one last cultural factor I must touch on—that is, culture change. Much has been written in Anthropology about how cultures change over time due to new technology, new ideas, increased migration, and political upheaval. A classroom is in some degree an interaction of cultures similar to the larger society and is also changing. The teacher's preferred symbols and art, his or her ways of seeing and organizing, attitudes towards the self and others, their hierarchy of values may be staying the same but the students of another generation may be learning all these variables in different ways. This force for change takes place in that structural institution we call school culture, with its values about order, discipline, and learning, and the amount of innovation tolerated in each subject taught. The math, science, language, social studies or the different arts each has a cluster of values around it, so students experience a change in cultures even as they move from one subject to another and all these subjects are affected by change as well.

If girls are raised differently than boys and women's culture is different from men's, then girls and boys will react somewhat differently to change. This doubles the complexity of all the variables we have been discussing.

Each classroom nucleus is itself set in the dynamics of nationwide and worldwide culture change. Childrearing varies as family structures are redefined by women's new role options. More people live in less space which demands better design and respect for other people's privacy. We are recognizing that our uses of our environment and resources must be sustainable if we are to survive. The increase in cultural diversity and culture change needs recognition to preserve social and political order and human dignity, whatever the cultural complex. As teachers we are faced with balancing our understandings about ethnic and cultural groups with our concern for the individual student. Descriptions of a cultural group are not fully definitive of any one child or small group.

Let me share with you the insights of an Educational Anthropologist, Harry Wolcott. Over 25 years ago he did his field work being a teacher in a Kwakiutl Indian school in British Columbia, Canada. His original question was "Why do so many Indian children fail in school?" In the intervening years, he has studied the effects of cultural differences between a children's culture and their school culture. Now he asks different questions. He wants to know what each child's particular vision of the world is and what are the cultural realities they have grown up with. He wants to know what they know and what it takes to get their attention. He cautions us to learn what individual children learn as well as the general knowledge of their group (Wolcott, 1989).

Some Final Reflections

Our world is changing at two levels—technically, knowledge flows worldwide in minutes—so the world is shrinking in time. Culturally, more and more of the world's people are searching their cultural roots to reestablish and maintain their identity and sense of worth—so the world is expanding and diversifying.

When problems are compounded, when many new technologies and transitions are present, people and institutions tend to retreat to what is more familiar and more comfortable—to stay within their own culture. Yet our need to understand each other was never greater.

The visual arts are a central system of communication. Art is a mode of thinking as well as feeling. Everyone's art has something to tell us, even though we, from our perspectives, may justifiably reject some of its message. Everything in everyone's culture doesn't necessarily contribute to human rights or human dignity, particularly when people of many cultures live in close proximity. We all need to be aware of our own cultural values as we try to comprehend our students and prepare them for living in an evolving multi-cultural world.

To make Multi-cultural and Cross-cultural Visual Art Education meet the challenge of our changing world, its social and psychological foundations need more cross-cultural research. The study of art, art history, aesthetics criticism, design and composition need to include many more cultures. Study of children and youth should be in terms of the effects of culture on perception, learning, cognitive style and creativity. Students' art preferences and background cultures need to be comprehended.

Our large goal from my perspective is to help students live in multi-cultural societies, respecting their own background culture and its art as they learn to respect other's culture and other's art. But unless we give each child and young person the psycho-cultural options to learn from where they are, they will have little opportunity to reach this goal. Art teachers and the theorists and researchers who support them are the quiet, advanced guard in these days of cultural diversity and change because art is a basic language of this diversity in this visually symbolic information age.

References

Berry, J.W. (1980). Social and cultural change. In H.C. Triandis & R.W. Brislen (Eds.), *Handbook of Cross-Cultural Psychology. Social Psychology Vol. 5.* Boston, MA: Allyn and Bacon.

Bourdieu, P. (1984). *Distinction: A social critique of the judgment of taste.* Cambridge, MA: Harvard University Press.

Brislen, R.W. (1983). Cross-cultural research in psychology. *Annual Review of Psychology, 34,* pp. 363-400.

Geertz, C. (1983). *Local knowledge.* New York, NY: Basic Books.

Hofstede, C. (1984). Art and Value. In R. Redfield & M.J. Herskovits (Eds.), *Aspects of primitive art.* New York, NY: The Museum of Primitive Art.

Joseph, A. & Murray, V.G. (1951). *Chamorros and Carolinians of Saipan.* Cambridge, MA: Harvard University Press.

McFee, J. K. (1961). *Preparation for art.* Wadsworth Publishing Co., Belmont, CA. Second Edition, June 1970. Japanese Edition, 1967.

McFee, J. K. (1966). Society, art and education. Publication of *A Seminar for Research in Art Education*, Edward L. Mattil, Project Director and Editor, U.S. Office of Education Cooperative Project No. V-002, University Park, PA: The Pennsylvania State University, pp. 122-140.

McFee, J. K. (1971, Fall). Children and cities: an exploratory study of urban middle and low income neighborhood children's response to studying the city. *Studies in Art Education, 13*(1), 50-59.

McFee, J. K. & Degge, R.M. (1977). *Art. culture. and environment.* Wadsworth Publishing Company, Inc., Belmont CA. Second Printing (1980) (Adapted printing 1992). Kendall/Hunt Publishing Co., Dubuque, IA, paperback.

McFee, J. K. (1980). Cultural influences on aesthetic experience. In J. Condus (Ed.), *Proceedings: The International Society for Education Through Art* (pp. 45-52). 23rd World Congress, Sydney, Australia: Holt, Rinehart and Winston.

McFee, J.K. (1988). Cultural dimensions in the teaching of art. In F.M. Farley and R.W. Neperud (Eds.), *The Foundations of Aesthetics, Art, and Art Education.* New York: Praeger.

McFee, J. K. (1995). Change and the cultural dimensions of art education. In R.W. Neperud (Ed.), *Transitions in art education: content and context.* New York, NY: Teachers College Press.

McFee, J. K. (1996). Interdisciplinary and international trends in multicutural art education. *Journal of Multicultural and Cross-cultural Research, 14,* 6-18.

Tobin, J. J., Wu, D. Y. H., & Davidson, D. H. (1989). *Preschool in Three Cultures: Japan, China and the United States.* New Haven, CT: Yale University Press.

Wolcott, H. (1989). *A Kwakiutl village and school.* Prospect Heights, IL: Waveland Press.

Reprinted with by permission, USSEA, *Journal of Multicultural and Cross-Cultural Research in Art Education, 14,* 6-18.

7

ART IN SOCIETY AND CULTURE

Preparation for Art, 2nd Edition 1970

Child art is a part of man's art. Children use art as a means of learning about their society, symbolizing and organizing what they learn, and expressing their reactions to it. Art in society is the framework in which the perception-delineation theory operates. It identifies some of the processes of responding to art, the environment that stimulates art, and the ranges of children's individual differences in these processes. Teachers need to understand both the functions of art and the ranges of children's differences in art in order that *content* (the subject of art) and the *teaching method* (the ways used by a teacher to reach individual children) are synthesized in classroom practice. Part of the process of education is to prepare children not only to learn through art but to deal with the complexities of art in adult life. It is then necessary for children as well as teachers to understand art in its broad communication functions. The purpose of this chapter is to help teachers understand more about art in society and to transmit their understanding to children.

Art is one of man's major language systems, a means of communication—of sharing his experience with others. In Figure 2-1 we can recognize symbols from different cultures in history. Each gives us information about the culture. Art can communicate qualities of experience that cannot be put into words. By sharing experience, through verbal language and through art, man develops and extends social groups and culture patterns. His records of what he does give man reference points from which to reflect and further develop and refine his experience. Communication through art is one important means of cultural development. It takes place as information is passed from one generation to another and as children learn from art how to respond to life patterns within their own culture. Their own individual expressions in art help them organize the symbols they are learning and give them bases for

FIGURE 2-1. *Transmitting Ideas Through Art Forms, Jean Ray Laury.*

further learning. The amount and degree of symbolic creativity allowed children depends upon the values of the cultural group they live in.

What is Culture?

Culture consists of the learned, shared, and socially transmitted forms of adaptation of human beings to the environment, which includes the habitat, other people, and their creations. A culture is the pattern of living among a given group of people. The pattern is developed by the group's shared values, beliefs, and opinions on acceptable behavior. Within the pattern people have roles to play and work to do. The culture in part directs how children are trained and how beliefs and values are maintained from generation to generation. Culture includes education, religion, science, art, folklore, and social organization.

The term *culture* is used some of the time to describe a very large society such as "Western culture." Among the nations of Western Europe and the Americas, and the peoples from these areas in other parts of the world, there are traditionally shared beliefs and values that differentiate them as a whole from other large cultural groups. *Culture* is also used to describe small, somewhat isolated or homogeneous groups where the similarities among the people are more evident. In talking about American culture, we refer to the *core culture*, meaning those values and beliefs shared in some degree by a majority of Americans. Different regional, ethnic, and religious groups within the whole are called subcultures. These people share the core culture in part but also have a nucleus of values and beliefs and ways of behaving that sets them apart.

Differences in values and beliefs are expressed through language and art forms such as dress, architecture, and decoration. Without verbal and visual means of sharing these ideas, cultures could not evolve. While there are nonliterate cultures (those without written language), there are no cultures that are without art forms, however primitive, for communicating ideas.[1]

Art is involved in most of the processes of transmitting what man has learned of his adaptation to his environment. The purpose of studying art in different cultures is to give teachers a somewhat broader basis for understanding how art functions in society generally, and how its functions are varied in meaning and style in any one specific society that has an identifiable culture pattern of values and attitudes. A society is a group of people who are organized for some political or social purpose. They do not necessarily have the same culture. A nation may contain several cultures and subcultures.

Within a single classroom there may be children who represent varied subcultures, who have been taught differing values, beliefs, and models of acceptable behavior. Though some people assume that art is a universal language, there are differences in symbolic meaning and style that do not communicate the same things to people who do not understand the culture in which the art was produced.

The rural economically deprived child who moves to the city may find little meaning in the beautifully illustrated children's book designed to appeal to metropolitan upper-middle-class children. The Kachina doll may appeal to many children with different cultural backgrounds, but only to a Hopi child will it go beyond the "little human" or doll symbol and represent an ancestral spirit.

What Is Art?

Art, like man, is a complex changing phenomenon, difficult to define. Anthropologist Melville Herskovits says art can be thought of as "any embellishment of ordinary living that is achieved with competence and has describable form."[2] The describable form may be very primitive or very complex, depending on the art tradition of the culture and the ability of the individual artist.

Thomas Munro has made a comprehensive study of art, combining the development of philosophical and anthropological concepts with theories in art history. Looking for trends and patterns, he summarizes art as "...man-made instruments for producing psychological effects on observers, individually and socially. These include perceptual, imaginative, rational, cognitive and emotional responses; also the formation of attitudes towards certain kinds of action and belief. Works of art are so used and always have been, even when not consciously intended."[3] Munro sees art as always expressing "something characteristic of its age in general. It also expresses only part of its age."[4] This means that art grows out of its past culture but has qualities of the present.

Using Munro's functional definition of art helps us see that art is a strong form of communication that operates as values, attitudes, and beliefs are shared and carried from generation to generation, from artist to artist, and from one cultural group to another.

Bohannon, an anthropologist, writes that "...art is a...mode of analyzing cultural images for better communication and more subtle appreciation. Language and art...are methods of communication and cultural statement— of capturing the image and transmitting it...of symbolizing the world of things and of sensations that create the image behind communication, social life and all culture. Symbolizing is the basic capacity of mankind that makes all culture and progress possible."[5]

Language (or art) is the mold into which perception must be fitted if it is to be communicated. Language is important for the individual in becoming Homo "sapiens;" learning to communicate one's perceptions is part of the growing up process.[6] Art is one of the primary means through which groups of people can examine their own images.

Julian Huxley links art with science and religion as one of the three main fields of man's creativity: "The essential function of the arts is one of bearing witness to the wonder and variety of the world and of human experience ...it is to create vehicles for the effective expression and communication of complex emotionally charged experiences, which are of value in the process of human fulfilment."[7]

The following working definitions of *art* and *child* art may be useful:

Art

Art is that form of human behavior by which man purposefully interprets and enhances the quality or essence of experience through the things he produces—from the simple enhancement of a tool to the expression of his deepest feelings and profound projections in painting, sculpture, architecture, and city planning. Art is one of man's basic means of communication—sharing the essence of experience from man to man and from generation to generation.

Man's art enhances his experience, and his experience enhances his art. This reciprocal action may lead to aesthetic and cultural growth.

Child Art

The child uses art to communicate (to himself and to others) his interpretation of his interaction with his environment. His art enhances his experience, giving him opportunity to develop and relate his growing concepts and ideas. His experience enhances his art, giving him new ideas to express. When a child responds to and through art he uses his abilities to remember, to visualize, to symbolize, to see likenesses and differences. The use of the language of art is a major avenue for learning—a key tool in education.

Sources of Taste

Man's like-dislike behavior in response to art forms ranges from unqualified acceptance or rejection to the most complex analysis of art forms with many different criteria. Judgment may be made in terms of the object's (1) place in art history, (2) uniqueness or creative quality, (3) communicative function in society, (4) emotion-arousing impact, (5) design or composition, or (6) technical quality.

Taste, with which a person makes judgments, develops within a given personality growing in a given cultural milieu. The individual's response is related to the personality structure he has developed, affected usually by the values and attitudes of his group. The commonly heard statement, "I know what I like, but I don't know why I like it," usually means that the individual has learned his preferences unconsciously. A person may prefer a ranch to a contemporary functional house without being able to analyze all the factors that determine his preference.

In addition to forming tastes uncritically, we often listen to other people's statements of what should be liked or disliked and accept their prejudices without questioning them. For example, an art education book published before 1930 made this statement: "The use of blue and green together is not good." No reason was given. The principle was only an expression of an attitude that was current at that time. Now blue and green are used together in profusion. They have always existed side by side in nature. If a teacher accepts the book's statement as true, he might limit the alternatives that he would provide children about blue and green. Lacking confidence in the field of art and assuming that such choices could be clearly "good" or "bad" taste, he tries to teach what he considers to be right.

The teacher is a "taste-maker." He reinforces or opposes the child's acquired attitudes or, by encouraging him to explore the dimensions of design and color, helps him to develop confidence in his own ability to make judgments. The child expands his aesthetic awareness by observing the taste of other people. The like-dislike behavior of individuals of the same local ethnic, religious, social, or economic status will probably be more alike than those of other backgrounds.

Your tastes are your "own." An exploration of the tastes of your contemporaries will show you which attitudes you have adopted without examination and which have grown as a result of your own observation. The darkened area in Figure 2-2 symbolizes an individual's taste. As a member of a national culture, he shares some kinds of experiences with all his fellow citizens. Certain experiences will be of importance only to a smaller group—social, economic, or other. The individual is more or less strongly influenced by training and experience within the subgroups of which he is a part. As part of a socioeconomic class he shares the tastes and values of that group. He also may belong to an ethnic or religious subculture that is varied from the whole class. As an individual growing up he has interacted some-

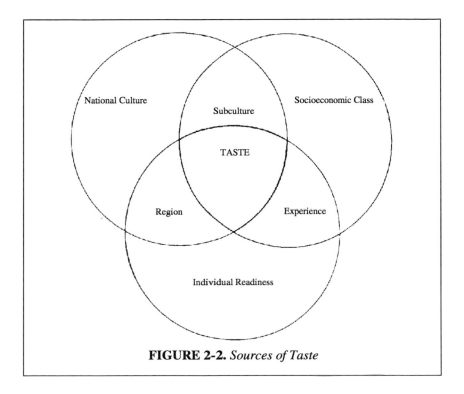

FIGURE 2-2. *Sources of Taste*

what differently from others with his subgroup or region, and so his experience has been unique.

The fine arts have sometimes been defined as expressive arts, and crafts or applied arts have been defined as enhancing arts. This dichotomy is losing its meaning. Expressive art products, such as paintings, sculptures, and prints, are not necessarily "finer" than ceramics, jewelry, and fabrics. Each individual product needs evaluation in terms of its relationships to other art forms with similar forms and functions. Many art objects are both expressive and enhancing; certainly some are higher in these quality than are others.

Functions of Art in Culture

Though art products vary widely in style and content, their communicative functions have similarities. Gerbrands, a Dutch anthropologist, has made a detailed review of the functions of art in culture of communicating the values, attitudes, and belief systems that evolve out of the interactions of persons within a society. He ranks the functions according to the frequency of their appearance among world cultures.[8] First is the expression of the "supernatural" in visible and tangible forms; second is the identification of different kinds of social status; third is the maintenance of political institutions; fourth is a structure for play. We will examine these functions as identified by other anthropologists.

First is religion or expressions of concepts of the supernatural.[9] In many cases the object of worship, a mask or carving, is considered to be animate— the thing worshiped, not just a symbol of it. The object's functions are to maintain the sense of reality shared by the members of the culture, to teach the religion to the young, and to hand it down from generation to generation.

Sand paintings show in visible form the Navajos' concepts of the nature of the world, its beginnings, the origins of man, and the whole complex myth system for maintaining their concepts of what is good and what is not good. The paintings are used as part of their ritual to help communicate the structure of their belief. In the healing ceremony, the medicine man uses the sand painting to create a feeling of direct contact between the patient and the "holy people." Not only does the patient see the visual symbol, he sits on it and is rubbed with sand from it. The ritual is a dramatic art form, the sand

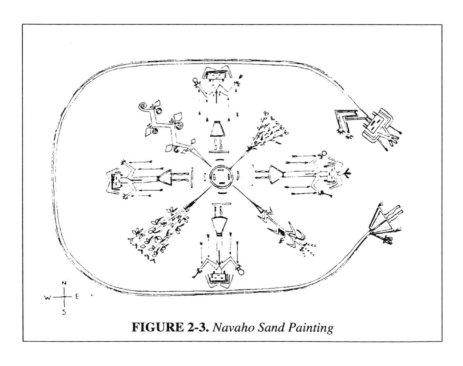

FIGURE 2-3. *Navaho Sand Painting*

painting a visual art form for maintaining their concepts of reality and training their children.[10]

Much art of the Romanesque, Gothic, and Renaissance periods was created to communicate religious concepts to the nonreading population. In our society a wide range of religious artistic symbolism exists. The churches that spread out from the Puritan tradition have had a standard of simple beauty. Often a single unadorned spire indicates a place of worship. By contrast, religions that use elaborate ceremonies have ornate churches with stained glass windows and altars rich in symbolic communication. With the advent of modern architecture the symbols of religious art have retained their meaning but changed their forms. All religions attempt to explain the nature of the universe—of reality.

The Kwoma people of New Guinea worship a *Marsalai*, a carved wooden idol. The artist who can make one has a position of prominence. The idol is used in secret societies, which in turn give continuity to the social organization of the group, give boys a means of achieving adult status through membership in the group, and separate the roles of the sexes. The men know that the Marsalai is only an idol, but women and small children live in fear of its power, though they never see it. The idol symbolizes an evil power that all the Kwoma fear. The fear holds the group together as a workable society. The abstract power becomes objective reality as an art form.[11]

These examples show how mankind uses art forms to give more meaning to interpretations of the nature of the universe. Language symbols alone are not enough, even for highly literate people. Nonliterate symbols are not stopped by the advent of written language. Physical scientists use models to illustrate their interpretations of the nature of the universe. The model is an ordered symbol used to communicate a structure of relationships representing time, space, size, and interaction in dimensions the layman can comprehend. Science and religion both use similar processes for communicating abstract concepts into symbols that can be looked at, manipulated, and touched.

The *second* most common function of art is to serve as an aid in identifying social position. The religious element may or not be present, but art objects can identify a priest or a medicine man. An art form may also identify a chieftain, a married woman, an unmarried woman, a believer, or a member of a clan, caste, or regional group. The art form may be a style of dress, jewelry, or body decoration with paint, feathers, furs, or fabrics. Status is identified both through variation in the art form and the symbolic status value of the material (see Figure 2-4). Women in Western civilization tend to prefer diamonds to shells to communicate their intended marriage, but in

105

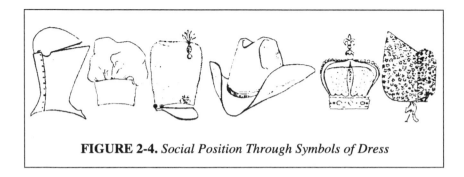

FIGURE 2-4. *Social Position Through Symbols of Dress*

nonliterate societies where diamonds have no known value shells may be much preferred.

The *third* function of art is maintenance of *political* stability. An art form may symbolize authority, show the boundaries of acceptable behavior, illustrate the results of law breaking, or induce fear of the supernatural to control behavior. In countries where the state dictates much of policy or a ruling class controls the art forms, art is used to teach doctrine, and the individual artist pursuing his own directions is suppressed.

The *fourth* function of art is play. Art contributes to entertainment and recreation. A costume may identify a play activity such as folk dancing, skiing, or swimming. Art may enhance objects used for play such as chessmen, playing cards, dolls, and toys. Satire, humor, and whimsy are found in art expression of the finest quality. Cartooning and illustration range from crude to elegant.

Identification of what is work and what is play is nebulous. A child may playfully manipulate paint for the fun of watching what happens; at another time the same child may use the same medium to communicate seriously an experience he has had. Is he playing or is he working?

In all its functions art provides aesthetic pleasure; its organization of forms elicits a sense of beauty. Art *enhances the experience* of people responding to or using the art form whether for religion, identification of social status, political maintenance, or play.

All of these functions help us learn about a culture through its art forms as well as through its written or spoken language. We use art to communicate who we are and how our culture works. So do all groups of people. We can then add a fifth main function of art in culture. When we look at all the functions of art in culture we find that art has an overall communication function. It is a form of cultural language.

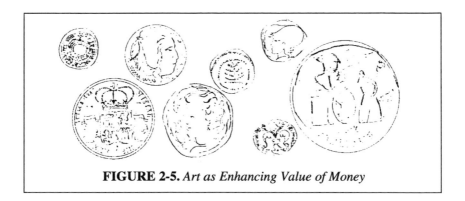

FIGURE 2-5. *Art as Enhancing Value of Money*

Have you ever wondered why we decorate money? Why do we go to the great cost of minting coins and engraving currency? Apparently decoration gives added meaning. From ancient times to the present we have enhanced the value of money by decorating it with symbolic forms (Figure 2-5). We use images of our cultural heroes, our mottoes of faith, and our national seal to authenticate the worth of a coin. The decoration of baskets, pottery, tools, and implements indicates a need of mankind to enhance the appearance of

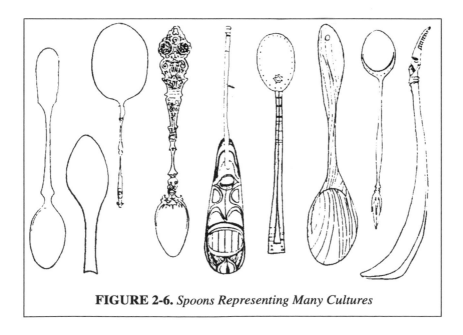

FIGURE 2-6. *Spoons Representing Many Cultures*

things he uses. Where the symbols used are part of the folklore, the enhancement has direct value in maintaining the culture.

The spoon designs in Figure 2-6 have their roots in different periods. In our culture, where we have borrowed the symbols and styles of so many periods, the ideas in our ornamentation have often lost their original meanings. We have collected from all over the world, mixing and adapting decorations as fashions changed, at the same time inventing our own forms, as any culture does.

As forms of communication and historic record, the arts help maintain culture. Even after long periods of time we can learn much about another people by studying its art forms. The Egypt of the Pharaohs seems remote in space and time, yet we can see and touch the tools, the buildings, the jewelry, the calendars, the mummies, and the religious artifacts that have been so well preserved. Many museums throughout the world have objects from this ancient culture. We can achieve empathic understanding of those remote people by studying the ways they enhanced their lives. We share in some degree the quality of their experience as we respond to their art forms.

If we can do this with groups remote in time and space, think of the cultural impact of learning and experiencing from one generation to another in the same culture. A small child walking down a city street learns visually about his culture. The kinds of buildings mean different kinds of functions; libraries, post offices, and court houses are impressive in size and in importance to his life. What people wear tells what they are—policemen, big boys, dignified people, undignified people, soldiers, sailors, businessmen in tailored suits, and grocers in aprons. The three-year-old boy who said "Ladies wear dresses and mothers wear jeans" was observing that costume defines occupation and role. Displays in windows, billboards, signs on telephone poles, theater marquees, all teach him about his culture.

The homes, the implements, and the decorations children see are constructed in conformity with the social organization, the beliefs and traditions of their groups. Clothing and body decoration indicate status. The manner of dress, nearly always differing between the sexes, may change from childhood to adulthood. Wearing "make-up" is a sign of "growing up." In another culture, body painting of another kind, or tattooing, may indicate an adult role—social position, occupation (warrior or medicine man), or tribal affiliation.

Enculturation through Art

A child is learning about the cultural values of his society from his earliest years. The symbols of what is considered to be important, the interpretation of reality, the status and roles of people and institutions, and the symbols of the political system are learned through observing adults' attitudes and behaviors toward them. The art forms used in play are particularly important in the enculturation process, the way a child learns about his own culture.

A child is prepared for adult roles through the things he is given to play with. In some societies sex role learning is introduced early through differences in toys considered appropriate for boys or girls. Adults in other societies do not differentiate children's toys until middle or late childhood. Toys that imitate adult roles are found in many societies. The form and symbolism used to make or decorate them is often the key to the relationship, as the toys are limited in the degree they actually work.

Most of this learning is vicarious. The child is not aware of his learning, and so he is not in a position to evaluate what he learns or to realize that art is a language that he is responding to. These functions can be made more explicit in art education. By studying the functions of art in other cultures and the ways other children learn about their cultures, pupils in a classroom can become more aware of the things they are learning through art about their own culture.

One function, which educators and artists may consider important, has been left out of this study of art in culture. That is the role of the individual in society and the ways he uses art as a means of interpretation of or reaction to the culture of his society. Most of the study of art in society does not deal with the individual, the ways the child creates his own synthesis or reactions to what he is experiencing. By learning to compare the varied work of artists in the same culture, children can learn more of the role of the individual and the possibilities he has to use art to communicate. Wayne Dennis, a psychologist who has worked closely with cultural anthropologists, has studied children's art products and finds that they are good resource materials for studying the values of a culture.[12] By comparing the drawings of children from one society with one culture to those of children from another society with another culture, he has identified differences in values that are illustrated by differences in symbols and organization of drawings. Comparisons have also been made in studies of the differences in drawings among children from different cultures within the same society.

109

Functions of Art in Contemporary Society

Gerbrands made his study mainly in nontechnical societies. During this period of mass media, advertising, packaging of products, and intensive growth of cities, some new adaptations of the functions of art are developing.

Enculturation of Children Today

The children in today's world are bombarded with art forms that are used to increase the exchange of goods and services. All the cultural functions of art are brought into play. On television an artificial portrayal of the "good life" is given the appearance of *reality*. Advertisements present the assumption that everyone wants the same quality of life and that particular products will most quickly and pleasurably provide the feeling or essence of that life. Actors perform roles appropriate to the "good life," display objects used to achieve status, take part in acceptable forms of play. Commercial art is used to enhance the quality of experience by suggestion.

Through the design of packaging, coffee becomes the brew of kings, hair spray the magic potion of youth and beauty, and a package of detergent a man who helps in a lady's kitchen. Television sets the pace and suggests the values, which are reinforced on the shelves of supermarkets. Never before in the history of mankind have so few people, the selectors and dispensers of mass media, communicated to so many.

Before the advent of mass advertising, the development and maintenance of cultural values and attitudes were done by some kind of social leadership through government or religion. The main function of education was to teach values to the coming generations. In an ideal democracy the values of government would reflect the values of the people, as those values evolve through the democratic process. Ideal education contributes to the development and maintenance of values, representing the general agreement achieved by the interaction of all segments of society. One such value is freedom of choice for the individual. The role of the school in relation to this value is to enable children to explore the range of alternatives in choice making and to analyze qualitatively the consequences of possible decisions.

Now another form of cultural leadership has emerged to influence values and taste. The transmission of cultural reality becomes less the domain of government, religious systems, and the teachings of elder members of the community. Culture is dispersed by directors of mass media programming and advertising. They select content for the most extensive and penetrating communications known to man; they select values they assume will offend the smallest numbers and entice the largest numbers of people. A national mediocrity ensues as they educate by indoctrinating rather than by encouraging critical thinking; they teach by contributing to conformity rather than by encouraging critical evaluation of many alternatives, so necessary to a dynamic society. Never before have all segments of the population, all age groups, been exposed to one large general source of information. The enculturation of children into the dominant society begins when they are infants, on the same bill of fare as adults.

Contributors to the Visual Environment

Among other contributors to the national scene are building contractors and private citizens who may or may not be concerned with their contribution to the community, now or in the future. The long tradition of the rights of property seems to carry with it the assumption that people do not see beyond property lines, so that if a person wishes to create ugliness or monotony it is his right as long as he stays on his own land. As populations grow and the ugliness of cities becomes more intolerable, changes in cultural values will have to take place. Education is needed to help people take responsibility for their contributions.

While some builders use art in a superficial manner, other more humanistic architects, designers, planners, and landscape architects are attempting to bring order and fundamental meaning to the environment through the things they provide the public. Renewal and rebuilding are done with the range of life patterns and values of the people in mind. The quality of the experience of people who walk down a city street, turn a corner to view a new vista, or sit waiting for a bus is considered. The need for renewal and recreation is considered in the design of a few motels and resort areas.

On a smaller scale, some package designers conceive of the product as it functions in someone's home rather than how it will get a consumer's attention in a store. Some advertisers are concerned about their tremendous responsibility as they transmit values and attitudes to children and youth. Though there are significant beginnings in these directions, responsible commercial designers are a minority in the face of all building and advertising that is going on.

Ethnic and Regional Contributions

In a modern cosmopolitan society like the United States, there are many ethnic, economic, and regional subcultures, and the range of art forms representing these different and overlapping cultures is extensive. The art work of people from many cultures contributes to the visual environment, with many different forms of ethnic symbolism giving richness and color. In architecture Greco-Roman and Gothic styles have come to us through the dominant core of American history and culture. The Spanish colonial influence is found in buildings in the Southwest, and has been borrowed in other parts of the country. Native materials were used by the American Southwest Indians long before the Spanish arrived, and adobe has been adapted to present-day use. Wherever Orientals have grouped together within larger cities, their own symbolism, religious artifacts, and social groups have developed and are still evident. The Scandinavian influence in what is called Sawn art or Carpenter's art flourished in the late nineteenth and early twentieth century in America. Many communities have a rich heritage of Scandinavian homes where a great deal of individuality has been expressed within a general style. America's own ranch house, which grew out of the simplest architectural form, still symbolizes the independent landowner to many people. Dutch and German influences in Pennsylvania, French influence in Louisiana, all contribute to the architectural diversity in the American environment.

Contributions to Change

One of the problems of the city today is confusion about symbols. The clusters of immigrants of the late nineteenth century could not change the architecture they found in the United States, but they soon produced symbols through the objects they sold in their community stores, in the ways the objects were displayed, and in the artifacts in their churches and homes that gave them a sense of identity. For many years homogeneous groups maintained environments in which ethnic symbols had meaning. Now many people have left the areas of their origins and have been absorbed into middle-class society, leaving their symbols behind. The present occupants of many of these older areas do not have the feeling of identity with the places that earlier residents had. The continued decay of old buildings and the lack of a distinct visual symbolic system on the part of the new inhabitants (except that which is given them by mass media) contribute to the decline of ethnically distinctive areas. In many cities such areas become slums.

We do not know whether the immigrants of the nineteenth century would have developed the sense of community they did if in every home there had been a television set telling them what symbols they had to have to live "the good life."

If we look at our cities and smaller communities from the standpoint of visual impact irrespective of the cultural history, we get a picture of what we in our haste for expansion, for progress, have produced. For some Americans the art forms of their community are decaying buildings, dark dreary streets, refuse. For others the art forms are gas stations, telephone poles, flashing neon signs, and billboards. Some Americans observe the harmonizing effect of shade trees in summer and the stark reality of unpainted disrepair of homes and bare trees in winter. Others live in monotonous but clean and neat housing areas. Some have inherited carefully planned villages whose quality may or may not be maintained. In areas of natural splendor the man-made hamlets are sometimes clusters of ugliness, as if the assumption were made that people look at nature, not the town.

The Expressive Arts in Contemporary Society

Rapid communication affects painting and sculpture. The most exploratory artists search for "reality" in new dimensions of expression. A new trend or form of experimentation takes hold in art centers like New York or Los Angeles and it is quickly amplified and extended to other regions. Some university art departments are becoming regional art centers, bringing in artists-in-residence, and sending their own staff to other centers to increase the stimulation of creativity. In the artists' search for reality, styles change rapidly: "op" artists explored man's reactions to experimental perceptions; "pop" artists forced us to look at the ingredients of our society—hot dogs, soft-drink bottles, and comic strips; formal abstractionists and abstract expressionists continue their experiments, while other artists return to stark realism or to the basic structure of things as they construct abstractions of underlying parts of things. In psychedelic art the artist tries to reproduce the immediate reality of artificially induced states of consciousness. Kinetic art consists of constructions based on inner muscular feeling.

The speed of interchange of ideas does not change the function of the artist's search for reality, but interchange appears to accelerate changes in style and focus. In small cohesive societies and in large authoritarian systems the artist's function is to express the values of the controlling group. One of the great values of the individual exploratory artist in a democracy is that his work, as a form of free speech provides yet another mirror for society to reflect upon itself. At the same time artists are not entirely separate from some segments of the culture of a complex society, and the art of a given period does give clues to the general values upheld.

The Subcultures of Artists

Among people who are concerned with some specific phase of the visual arts, there are subcultures and subgroups. All painters, all designers do not have the same values. It is important for the classroom teacher to recognize these groups so that he can understand the works that they produce and evaluate them in terms of the artists' value systems. Then a teacher can better evaluate his own goals for children in art. An artist may be working toward the values of some subculture among art groups and ignoring others, or toward some subculture of the society itself, which may or may not be appropriate for school children.

In almost every region there are groups of painters who organize themselves to preserve the naturalism of their area against the inroads of "modern" art on the one side and the art of products and commerce on the other. There are also weavers, potters, and other craftsmen who preserve regional traditions in fabrics, ceramics, glass, and leather goods. Examples are found in Appalachia, New England, and the Southwest. In many areas traditional crafts of needlework in varying degrees of quality are displayed at county and state fairs.

Craftsmen throughout the country who are experimental and creative in their work are developing national as well as regional qualities in their art. National and regional craft shows set new standards of excellence of design and establish new bases for uses of tools and materials. The craftsmen are as interested in the expressive impact and the design quality of their work as they are in the craftsmanship.

"Sunday painters" or nonprofessional artists have shows throughout the country. Sidewalk exhibits, art festivals, and community exhibits are organized for people who use their leisure for work in art. The work that is displayed ranges from copies of other paintings or photographs to work that is accepted in juried exhibitions.

The professional artist may work alone or he may be a member of a group of artists. He may be a teacher in an art school, a public school, a college, or a university art department. He may be working within some "school" of art—that is, a style of art of a philosophical framework. The quality of work among professionals varies widely. Though one school of art may be most popular at any given time, excellent artists within different schools maintain recognition in the art world.

There are many artists in industry—designers of fabrics, furniture, automobiles, appliances, printed matter, packages, products, interiors, costumes, and stage sets. In fields in which a few manufacturers control production the range of design is not great—particularly in automobiles and appliances. In furniture, fabrics, and publishing the range of quality is very great, from furniture built for quick turnover to furniture designed for gracious use and durability, from fabrics designed to catch attention to those that enhance the use of clothing or interiors, from pulp magazines to masterworks in graphic design. Awards for excellent design, exhibits of outstanding commercially produced products, and some excellent schools of design in art schools and universities are pace-setters. The great need is for a general public that is aware of the functions of design and that has developed some degree of discrimination.

Professional architects, landscape architects, urban designers, and city planners are found throughout the country. Some are conservative, preserving traditions; others break with tradition to establish new directions for environmental design. Still others try to achieve an environment that respects both the past and its contribution to the quality of the present and the accelerating demands for change. Designers must plan aesthetically and realistically for the burgeoning population and for the technical change that is upon us. They must create attractive spaces for the identifiable environment of the individual and small group as well as for the mass of society as people move within and without the structure of cities, traffic patterns, and rural areas.

The Need for Perceptual Education

One reason the language of art may be so suddenly complex for many students is that most of us were educated in terms of concepts. Few of us have learned adequately to look visually and, further, to look at art in its broad forms as language communicated through its visual qualities. We have learned what things are, how they relate to other things, and we have learned enough visual characteristics to identify objects. We have not been exposed to the study of the visual world as language, with its different cultural meanings, nor have we been taught its grammar, which is design. We have seen art as something apart from life rather than as an integral part of it. But even though we may not have been critically aware of art's functions, our visual environment has influenced the quality of our experience and in many cases our decisions. The artist and the designer are sometimes not recognized for their influence on the environment, nor are their services always utilized, because the public often has no conscious concern for the effect of the environment on the quality of existence. The rather sudden national anxiety about the visual quality of our cities and about our refuse-strewn natural environment has apparently risen because the situation has become so bad that it can no longer be ignored. Our perceptual world is now becoming part of our conceptual world.

A Clarification of Terms

A *percept* is an impression of an object obtained by use of the senses. A *concept* is an idea about an object, generalized from previous experiences with the object. To illustrate, let us assume that we are observing a late model automobile. If we depend upon concepts mainly we look for cues to identify the maker, the model, the color, and the key symbols the designer has used to identify this model and make from other models and makes of cars. If we have been trained to respond to the percepts presented by the automobile we see all the changing contours as we walk around the machine. We see many variations in the color as reflections, and lights change the visual image of the original pigment color that was sprayed on. What shape is a car? The more concept-oriented person tends to have a generalized stereotype of the for The person who is visually sensitive realizes that there are as many different visual images of the form as there are positions from which he can view the automobile. In other words, perceptual reality and conceptual reality are not necessarily the same—but they can be combined when the concepts a person has cover all the variations in visual reality as well.

Our concepts come from what we know about things, our percepts from our ongoing scanning of things. Some persons observe within the limits of their concepts; others are open to new percepts which, by giving them more information, require them to increase the richness and variety of their concepts. As individuals attend to more visual information they develop more concepts for sorting and organizing the visual information. There is considerable evidence that learning is required in seeing, so one of the responsibilities of the teacher is helping children acquire more visual awarenesses and concepts with which to think about what they see.

Implications for Teachers

Where is the elementary school teacher to find himself in this vast world of art? Teachers usually have extensive backgrounds in the other language systems, beginning with their own training as children. The language of vision has not been stressed in schools, art has not been seen as a major form of communication at the same time that art forms have been overwhelmingly introduced into the mainstream of modern civilization. The discrepancy is between the accelerating intensity of the influences of visual communication, on the one hand, and the lack of ability to analyze and criticize either the message or the form through which it is projected, on the other.

A key purpose of this book is to help teachers bridge this gap, to help them see the so-called fine arts and children's art in the broader context of communication and culture. A second purpose is to help teachers to understand the grammar of vision, so that they may help children become more visually literate and sensitively aware, both to what is projected to them through the broad arts and to their own creations and contributions to society. To help children, teachers need more understanding of human behavior in art, design in art products, and factors that influence choices. A third purpose is to help teachers understand the ranges of readiness that children in different socio-economic, ethnic, and geographic areas may have for perceiving, for becoming aware, for solving problems creatively, and for expressing their ideas.

Summary

Art is a major language system of society. Through art man can share his experience with other men, and groups of men can communicate their shared values and attitudes, their culture, with other groups of men.

A society can be made up of one culture or many, with each subculture developing art forms that are somewhat different from the others. Some societies have a core culture that is shared in part by the subcultures of the society.

There are many definitions of art, but most include the points that art interprets, enhances, and communicates man's experience. The child uses art to interpret and enhance his experience to himself and others. It gives him a tool for symbolizing and learning.

An individual's taste or aesthetic judgment is learned in his national culture, his own particular subculture, and his unique experience as a developing individual.

The major functions of art in society are to maintain the sense of reality of the culture's belief system, to identify the status and roles of people and institutions, to maintain political institutions, and to enhance and structure aspects of play.

Children learn about their culture through art, and by being exposed to adults' reactions to art forms. Art is also a way for them to respond individually to society.

In today's society, much of children's learning about culture comes to them screened through television and other mass media; the transmission of cultural values to the young has shifted more to media specialists, rather than the family and other social organizations. A sameness about culture is learned.

Our cities and towns reflect the various cultures that have contributed art forms to our society. But neglect and decay are turning our cities into dark and dreary places. Styles in the expressive arts change with great rapidity as society changes. Artists have many roles in this society, but their contributions are not generally recognized.

All of these forces in society point up to the need for perceptual as well as conceptual literacy and emphasize the challenge to teachers to help children cope with the complexity of change in society through understanding the functions of art.

Notes

[1]Ralph L. Beals and Harry Hoijer, *An Introduction to Anthropology* (New York: The Macmillan Company, 1953), p. 538.

[2]Melville Herskovits, *Cultural Anthropology* (New York: Alfred A. Knopf, Inc., 1955), p. 235. Reprinted by permission.

[3]Thomas Munro, *Evolution in the Arts* (Cleveland: The Cleveland Museum of Art, 1963), p. 419.

[4]*Ibid.*, p. 492.

[5]Paul Bohannon, *Social Anthropology,* Chapter 3. (New York: Holt, Rhinehart, & Winston, 1963).

[6]*Ibid.*, p. 48.

[7]Julian Huxley, "Evolutionary Humanism," in *New Bottles for Old Wine* (London: Chatto and Windus 1957), p. 306.

[8]A. A. Gerbrands, *Art as an Element of Culture, Especially in Negro Africa* (Leiden: E. J. Brill, 1957).

[9]*Ibid.*, p. 131.

[10]Clyde Kluckholn and Dorothea Leighton, *The Navajo* (Cambridge: Harvard University Press, 1956), p. 151.

[11]John W. M. Whiting, *Becoming a Kwoma* (New Haven: Yale University Press, 1941), pp. 215-216.

[12]Wayne Dennis, *Group Values through Children's Drawings* (New York: John Wiley & Sons, Inc., 1966), p. 210.

By permission, *Preparation for Art*, Second Edition. Belmont, CA: Wadsworth. Copyright June King McFee.

8

DEFINING ART EDUCATION IN THE EIGHTIES

NAEA Super Session, Chicago, 1981

The charge I have been given for this paper is to define the field of art education as I see it functioning in the context of this decade. I shall attempt this by focusing on six questions: What do we art educators do that is the same? What different goals do we pursue and how do our differences and likenesses fit together as a field? Upon what other fields do we depend? How do we teach? Where do we teach? How may social and political changes in this decade affect what we do?

Several tasks are required to answer these questions: The *first* is to identify the most central and shared operations which art educators use to reach their diverse goals. What do we all do that is alike? What gives art education a central identity and holds our diversity together?

The *second* task is to identify the current major goals of our field as they in turn relate to content to the individual and to society. As we complete this task we can begin to see who we are even though we may vary widely in our practice of the shared operation. Then we have tentatively completed the first and second tasks we have identified in some degree the central network of art education as it is operating at this time.

The *third* task is to identify the fields and disciplines we draw upon as we develop our different goals. They may include different aspects of philosophy, and aesthetics, the history and practice of art, architecture, and the fields contributing to educational theory.

The *fourth* task is to identify the different teaching methodologies or strategies that we may use to teach toward any of our goals.

The *fifth* task is to identify the institutions we depend upon to carry on our field and that affect how we reach our goals. They include pre-schools, elementary and secondary schools, art museums, galleries, community and rehabilitation centers, colleges and universities, etcetera. Each of these is a network of roles, practices, values and environments which influence what we do.

In the *sixth* task we must continually evaluate the social and political forces that may affect us and the institutions through which we operate. Within the limits of this short paper I will deal with each of these tasks briefly.

First: *The Shared Operation*

In the *first* defining task let me suggest that the *shared* operation, the things we all do in common, that holds the diversity among us together and that differentiates us from other fields is as follows: Visual art education takes place when one person with some competence in visual art and education, affects through teaching, the way another person apprehends or produces visual art. This response in turn affects the teacher. Thus the teaching role involves a social action and reaction. The teacher and student may be consciously aware of the impact or not.

The shared operation allows us a great deal of flexibility in practice through the different definitions of words used, such as what we include in art, or as education. It is in operation whether the teachers' competence is in criticizing and analyzing art or in producing art or both. It includes all the different ideas of what the content is studio arts, fine arts, crafts, electronic arts, art criticism, aesthetics, popular arts, museum arts, art as social commentary, environmental arts, cross-cultural arts. It doesn't limit us to any age or kinds of individual need as long as our shared operation is going on.

The overall, ongoing network of art education is held together by this common operation. It is maintained by those people who, by practice of it and by social definition, are the teachers or influencers of other people in their response to and expressions through art. It is used by people using all the current goals and will allow for change as new goals develop.

Second: *Different Goals*

The *second* defining task is to describe the different goals that overlap the shared operation but are also different from each other due to the individual art educators values. Some of the different goals of art educators include teaching art through: manipulating traditional and emerging media; solving design problems; learning critical skills; developing aesthetic awareness; comparing art cross-culturally. Also by fostering: child development; increasing creative expression; actualizing the self; analyzing value expression; changing society *through* art. Some of these goals lead us to be more concerned with the content some more with the individuals we are teaching and some more with the role of the visual arts in society. In some degree we are all concerned with each of these perspectives. All of these areas of goals cluster around the shared operation and make up the complex network that we call art education. Reviewing such points of view illustrates that art education is a complex web of inter-related people, content, practice, and values—each drawing upon somewhat different other fields.

Third: *Relationships to Other Fields*

In the *third* defining task we identify the relations of our field to other fields and disciplines. This depends on the other fields our goals draw upon and the institution through which we work. For example, a museum educator would have to be very knowledgeable about content, but could draw more upon art history, art criticism, or upon aesthetics. At the same time he or she may be most concerned about the social functions of museums, to enhance the quality of life in the community and apply their particular concern for content to the general attitudes of the members of the community toward visual art. This requires particular understandings from sociology and anthropology.

One high school art teacher may be very concerned that the visual arts be recognized as intellectual problem-solving and put her major focus on developing curricula that enables learners to comprehend major concepts, relationships and aesthetic values expressed in art. This requires that she understand aspects of information and learning theory as well as aesthetics. The teacher in the next room may be deeply concerned with the impact of mass media and its emphasis on vicarious experience on adolescents. He may push his students into intense, direct analysis of its impact in their own lives, to develop critical skills and to express this thorough art media. This teacher should have background in advertising and cognitive psychology as well as design.

An elementary art consultant who values art as a fundamental experience in children's cognitive, conceptual, perceptual development tries to relate research in cognitive and developmental psychology to the formulation of art curricula that provides growing opportunities for individual children.

A college art professor may be concerned with the computer as a graphic tool and as a means for increasing students' options in expressing their ideas. This requires background in computer technology, computer theory, as well as visual design.

A professor of art education may prepare teachers to utilize all aspects of art education or limit their curriculum to one point of view. In any case, teacher preparation in art draws on an interdisciplinary base. In some degree each of these people is using the shared operation, has goals that relate to some aspects of the content of art, some concerns for individual students, and has some social purposes of art. Each of these clusters utilizes somewhat different combinations of foundational networks. These include:

Art and Design	Sociology of Art
Environmental Arts	Popular Culture Studies
Art History	Cultural Anthropology
Art Criticism	Developing Technologies
Aesthetics	Learning Theory
Experimental Aesthetics	Cognitive Psychology
Philosophy	Curriculum

Psycho-Social Foundations of Education and Art Education

Fourth: *Teaching Strategies*

In the *fourth* task we identify the most used methodologies or strategies for teaching art. While all of us do some teaching, we may focus more on an individual instruction method, an exploration and creativity based method, a self-expression method, an analytical problem-solving method, an inquiry method, a behavioral objective method, a social interaction method, or a directed learning method. Any content area can be taught with any teaching strategy though some strategies are more useful in reaching some goals than others.

Fifth: *Institutional Support*

In the *fifth* task we identify the ways our goals and our shared operation fit with the values of the institutions in which we practice art education. A majority of us are involved with teaching in the institutionalized forms of education, in pre-school, elementary, secondary and college and university settings. Depending on our work we are also involved in the network of these institutions—some of us more with one than the other. The nature of the institution affects how we relate art education to it and the goals we as individual teachers value and emphasize. People who teach art in other institutions such as in community and recreation centers, in museums and galleries, in prisons and hospitals, are related to the networks of these institutions. The kind of institution determines the age and selection of students, acceptable practices, requirements for teaching, structure of teaching/learning, time and space conditions, evaluation criteria, and facilities and the range of flexibility we have.

We have only briefly tapped the many kinds of goals and practices of art educators. They all in some ways influence the response of students to and through art. Each shares in some degree the larger network we call art education, and each draws on other networks in the broader field of art, art criticism and aesthetics, of education, of the social and behavioral networks that are foundational to education and to art. Each is influenced by the socio-cultural networks of the teaching situation they are in and the political environment that supports it.

Each part of the art education network is in a process of change. So are all the institutions and related networks that we apply to our field. Thus the process of definition needs to go on continuously.

Sixth: *Current Forces*

This leads us to the *sixth* defining task—identifying the current forces outside our central and related networks that may affect us in this decade. We see new shifts in national and world politics that may further affect the resources which are the economic support systems for almost all human endeavor. The impact on humanity, on the arts, on education are hard to project or comprehend. One comforting fact of history is that while some things change rapidly many things change slowly. But with all this uncertainty let me identify some of the things that appear to me to be descriptive of what the 1980s may portend, particularly for art education.

During this decade the numbers of economically deprived and ethnically diverse students will increase, due to less government support and increased immigration, while the research and program development to help teachers reach these students is decreasing. The burden on already burdened teachers will increase.

The lowered support for public education will tend to increase private education which contributes to a more stratified and less open society. The overall impact of this on society may lead to more elitism in the arts after years of effort to democratize the arts and make them available to all people. The commercialization of the arts through mass media will continue.

The impetus to save the old American cities which has made some headway in the last twenty years is now being drastically curtailed. As the quality of cities decreases the better educated and more affluent leave. Yet these older cities have been the crucible of the arts and higher education. Now they will be left with much less private or government support. Art education feeds on vibrant art movements, centers of aesthetic inquiry, and educational and social science research. This means that regional art and educational centers will have to take on more of the leadership roles in these areas even as they, too, are being cut back on support.

All of us are influenced by the nature of the material culture around us—the values expressed by the art and architecture and the value laden human-built environment in which both we and our students live and work. Our lives may well be affected as environmental quality controls are reduced. The need to prepare students to take aesthetic as well as social and economic responsibility for the shared environment will increase rather than decrease, as government support and concern for cities decreases. Yet we in art education have been slow in accepting this as one of our responsibilities. The contribution of education in the visual arts to qualitative survival when so many must use so much less in much more densely populated spaces, must be made clear.

Certainly the central theme of all this is that there will be much more responsibility placed on the professional networks of our society rather than on government. The art education network will be affected by these changes in every respect. Understanding our own complexity—tolerance for all the perspectives should enable us to draw on all those strengths—and enable us to reinforce our field and work together more effectively.

The insights and research that the Black, Indian and Asian art educators can bring to us should help all of us to teach more of our students. The weaknesses in our teaching of female students as identified by researchers among the Women's Caucus should help us make art education more universal. The materials being developed in the related fields, aesthetic education, the critical skills developed by those of us interested in the social aspects meaning and uses of art, and all the experimentation and development of the studio artists and craftspersons—the thousands of studies in psychology related to art and design in information processing, cognitive style, imagery, memory, creativity, and personality, the many developments in curriculum planning and teaching strategies—all these can contribute to our strengths as the forces on the outside further decrease our support.

As is common among people who share an operational practice with its network of ideas and values, social organizations are formed to maintain, direct the growth, direction, and communication between the various aspects of the network. A supporting organization such as the National Art Education Association becomes even more critical when not only ours but our related networks are threatened. But we may well need to increase communications within our professional organization so that the interactions between us are increased. We need not be divided between the doers and thinkers, the practitioners and theorists, the teachers of children and the teachers of adults. We all need to be more concerned with content, with the needs of different individual students and with the social meanings and impacts of the visual arts.

Further, the overall network of visual art education can be strengthened as different groups of us vary somewhat in the direction and degree of affiliation with other networks. All perspectives enrich our field and do not necessarily draw us out of it as some fear. If we use information from other fields effectively we haven't left our field for another field, we have only made useful connections. It can only strengthen us.

In a time of critical stress from outside our survival depends upon our recognition of the complexity and contributing strengths from all parts of our field. It requires comprehension of the relationships the parts have to the whole so we can make our position as a whole field more clearly recognized and supportable.

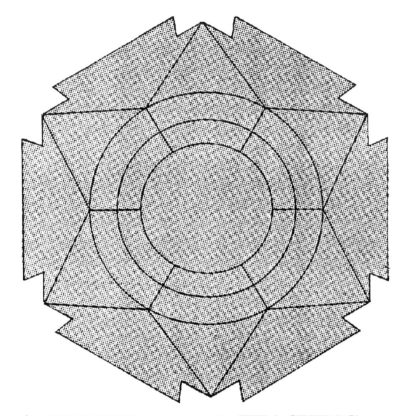

1 SHARED
OPERATION

2 DIFFERENT
GOALS

3 RELATIONSHIPS
TO OTHER
FIELDS

4 TEACHING
STRATEGIES

5 INSTITUTIONAL
SUPPORT

6 CURRENT
FORCES

Models by Martin Rayala.

1 SHARED OPERATION

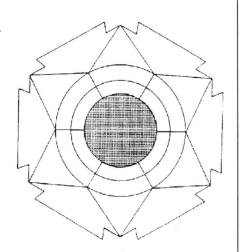

Visual art education takes place when one person with some competence in visual art and education affects through teaching the way another person apprehends or produces visual art.

This response in turn affects the teacher.

2 DIFFERENT GOALS

TEACHING ART THROUGH...
Manipulating media
Solving design problems
Learning critical skills
Developing aesthetic
  awareness
Comparing cross-culturally
Child development
Increasing creative expres-
  sion
Actualizing the self
Analyzing value expression
Changing society
  ...THROUGH ART

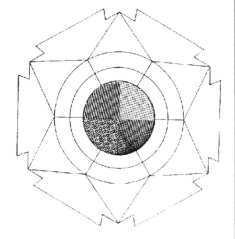

3 RELATIONSHIPS TO OTHER FIELDS

Art and Design
Environmental Arts
Art History
Art Criticism
Aesthetics
Experimental Aesthetics
Philosophy
Sociology of Art
Popular Culture Studies
Cultural Anthropology
Developing
    Technologies
Learning Theory
Cognitive Psychology
Curriculum
Psycho-Social Foundations

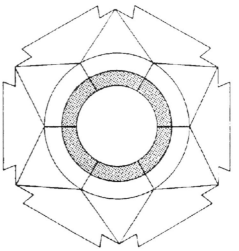

4 TEACHING STRATAGIES

Individual Instruction
Exploration & Creativity
Self-Expression
Analytical Problem-
    Solving
Inquiry
Behavioral Objectives
Social Interaction
Directed Learning

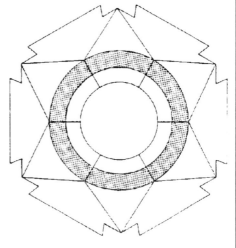

5 INSTITUTIONAL SUPPORT

Pre-Schools
Elementary
Secondary
Colleges and Universities
Community and
    Recreation Centers
Museums and Galleries
Rehabilitation Centers

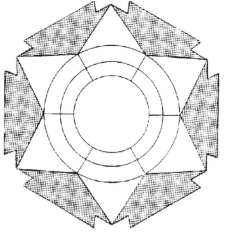

6 CURRENT FORCES

DECREASED GOVERNMEN-
    TAL SUPPORT
Increased economic and ethnic
    diversity
Decreased support for teaching
More teacher responsibility
Decrease in public and increase in
    private eduction
More class stratification
Less democratization of the arts
Decreased rehabilitation of major
    cities
Devitalization of art and knowledge
More responsibility on regional art and education centers
Decrease in environmental control
Decrease in environmental quality
Increased need for learning critical and qualitative skills
More responsibility put on professions increase communication networks in and
    between fields

Reprinted by permission of CSEA. From Defining Art Education, First Supersession Address NAEA Conference, Chicago, Illinois, April 1981. Published *Annual Journal: Canadian Society for Education Through Art*, 1986, vol. 17, pp. 7-12.

9

ART EDUCATION PROGRESS: THROUGH A FIELD OF DICHOTOMIES OR THROUGH A NETWORK OF MUTUAL SUPPORT

Studies Award Lecture NAEA, Kansas City, 1990

The challenge to prepare the *Studies* Lecture for 1990, combined with freedom from daily academic concern, has given me more opportunity to reflect on my perspective on art education. Like all of us living through this extraordinary period in world history, watching intense social, political, and cultural readjustments, while contemplating their implications for this society, has been impelling and stirring. We have been forced to reassess our basic assumptions about the world and our interrelations with it. It requires flexibility with ideas to see these evolving connections in this transitional social arena.

Not only the world scene but many aspects of our own society require rethinking. We are finally recognizing that this nation is far more diverse than we have been willing to accept; that minorities as a whole are no longer the minority in many urban areas; that the influx of new cultures is far greater than immigration data document; and that the basic ingredient of our society, the family is undergoing transitions which ripple affect society as a whole. Being off campus we have missed dialogue about these tumultuous events with colleagues and students. I have missed discussing their impact on art and education, so I particularly welcome this invitation and your reactions.

During my years of teaching, thoughtful graduate students often raised the questions "Just what is art education?" Trying to impress them with the importance of their own inquiry, my answer, in content, was "It is what we make it become." Years before, just after finishing my dissertation at Stanford, I went to an NAEA convention in New York City. There I first met Kenneth Beittel, and we shared our excitement with graduate research. He asked to take my dissertation to his great teacher Viktor Lowenfeld to read and then to meet with them the next morning. Lowenfeld's response was much the same—that we were in our infancy as a field and that many steps, including mine, were needed to develop it. He was encouraging about the inquiry I was pursuing This impressed me because, even though his perspectives were quite different than mine, his concepts of the field were more inclusive. It is in this more open context that I will pursue my presentation here.

Reflecting on the ideas that make up our field, I became concerned that we have become fragmented by clusters of dichotomous positions whose ends are viewed as mutually exclusive from one another. Depending on the viewer, if one position is right, the other must be wrong. My mental image was that we are going off in all directions and that we need to find out what can hold us and our positions together. Time away has helped me become more conciliatory and less polarized in my own convictions; it has encouraged me to look for interrelating factors that might hold us together as we develop art education. This is not meant to infer that all is relative and there are no criteria for assessing the value of each perspective. But pursuing one's own inquiry does not preclude consideration of the values of other traditions and developments in the field and the relation of our work to them.

I have been analyzing how dichotomies may become continua if viewed from a larger social context. In the process, I have come to believe that all positions in art education have some relevant application, that there is some degree of relationship between opposing views, and thus, that none are mutually exclusive from each other. On this basis, no position can stand alone; rather it becomes part of a network of possibilities that can be considered for teaching in this changing and diversifying cultural environment. I have long been concerned with the impact of society and culture on our field, but never before have they had such effect as they do today.

Now we will look at art education in terms of seven familiar areas of controversy or dichotomous positions, analyze their relations in terms of the impact of today's social and cultural change, and suggest implications for the field that emerge from this analysis.

Dichotomy 1. Western Fine Arts Versus Other People's Art

This dichotomy concerns Western fine art contrasted with multicultural, folk, and popular arts as represented in contemporary society. On one hand is the position that art means Western fine art in all its periods and which exists for its own sake as one of the keystones of Western culture, it should be taught to all students no matter what their background. On the other hand we have the assumption that in a democratic society the arts of all the cultures and of all social classes can be analyzed, critiqued, and accepted as art in terms of each group's value system. Some selectivity of subject matter appropriate for students of different ages would hold for these arts as it does for fine art.

Now we can begin to analyze the relations between these two points of view. The *first* the Western fine art position, by its criteria of selection is often interpreted to mean that all other arts are not worthy of inclusion as "real" art. The *second* a more anthropological view of art, also relates the judgment of what is art to the criteria developed by the people who create and support that particular art. But it respects the contextual validity of the arts of all groups, including Western fine art.

It would lessen the dichotomy if the criteria for deciding what is or is not art were separated from criteria of quality within a particular art tradition. When we look at the different arts in our society, we find that each is supported by a network of people who share the same values about the art, because it expresses their values. Thus they and the artists can be understood to comprise an art subculture. As teachers we need to be aware of an art subculture's criteria for deciding what is and is not art and its criteria for judging quality. Then we would recognize that the criteria used to accept and judge quality in an art tradition such as fine art is not necessarily appropriate in identifying any other art as acceptable and having qualities in its own context. An ideal education in art should enable individuals to be multicultural in their responses and understand many arts within their subcultural value systems, and thus have a more definitive basis for comparing them.

All art traditions have social value. What we describe in Western culture as "art for art's sake" usually functions in many social and individual ways. If art exists, it serves some purpose of communication and expresses social values as it feeds on and evolves from its own art subculture. Teaching about "art for art's sake" or any other art tradition as part of a particular culture helps students comprehend the functions of art in culture generally. This helps them gain a much broader yet culturally specific understanding of art.

Do not misconstrue my remarks to mean that I am rejecting Western fine art in education, but rather that it should be studied in terms of evolving

Western cultural values. This can help students from other art subcultures be more aware of the attitudes and values that have affected fine art and ways these continue to influence it as compared with the ways other arts are affected by changes in their art subcultures. This more relative approach allows students from other backgrounds to compare their art to fine art without rejecting their own.

One prevalent fallacy among people is to be so centric in socio-cultural views of art that they assume their responses, categories, and judgments are universal. Though centric views can be applied to other arts they need to be recognized as such, and other cultural systems for viewing art should be considered.

Perhaps some cultural informants—students recently arrived from other parts of the world, or students from folk, ethnic, or popular art backgrounds in this country—would critique Western fine art from their perspectives if they knew their art values would be respected. Then both we and they would develop a cross-cultural awareness of the quality and meaning of other arts.

Dichotomy 2. The Art Versus the Education of Art Education

Identifying the conflict over the importance of either art or education could help resolve much divisiveness in our field and help identify the relationships between art and education. On the one hand are those who are concerned with the *art* of art education and have little concern with how it is going to be taught and to whom. They assume that preparation to teach art should be primarily in content, and that enthusiasm and involvement with art is all that is needed to become a good teacher. At the other extreme are those who believe that preparation to teach art should be primarily in *education*—that is, ways to teach students with many different aptitudes for creating and responding to varying kinds of art.

Both these positions, art or education, have dichotomous subsets. For example, within the fine arts tradition there are opposing positions about the content of art. Some adhere to the position that learning about art, its history and its criticism, is far more important than having every little pupil in America learn to be a hands-on artist. Others, filled with the joys and triumphs of the creative experience, feel that every human being should have an opportunity to develop his or her art potential through direct involvement.

Those who stress education also have disagreements. The people emphasizing education can be divided among a vast array of theories about teaching. At one end you will find those who believe child-centered education never lost its importance and should be restored in schools today. Another group of people are returning to direct instruction and strict discipline to develop art skills and abilities. These two poles are based on ideological differences: the first, concern for students' individual differences and cultural backgrounds; the second, concern that they learn correctly what they need to know.

In considering the relationships within the main dichotomy (the art or the education of art education), we need to look at our own basic assumptions and backgrounds—how our culture, personality, and experience have channeled our interpretation of experience. Are we looking at the students in a given school or community and selecting as appropriate teaching our psychocultural perspectives on learning? These need to be self-recognized and evaluated when observing students and making decisions. The same holds true with our concepts of art. If we are more skilled in criticism than with clay, in computer-assisted than in free-hand, more concerned with folk, pop, gender-based than traditional fine arts, then these skills and related attitudes will affect our choices of what is appropriate for others. Being more aware of our biases, we can look at our decision-making more objectively, and give careful consideration to the broad ranges of art in this society and to the diversity in cultural aptitude and modes of learning appropriate for different student groups and individuals. All these modes and ways are avenues for learning about art, that can be extended and built upon.

It is possible that some students come from cultures where the only learning they know is by imitation, which for others would be coercive. To some with deep roots in this country, Western fine arts is as remote as if they had come from a non-Western culture. Thus it continues with the many variables found in art and among students. This does not mean that we cannot look at our society and where it seems to be going to set goals that we hope to achieve. But our means of setting and pursuing these goals need much flexibility within the repertoire of both the art and the education of art education.

Bridging the gap between these two dichotomous positions and turning them into a continua of related concerns has strong implications for teacher education programs. Ideally, departments should include faculty with a range of backgrounds in art, extensive backgrounds in art education theory, research, and supporting foundations in the social sciences and education. If productive and/or scholarly skills, and if excellence in both teaching and research are rewarded, then the art and education of art education can thrive together.

Dichotomy 3. To Expand or Maintain Our Field

Tendencies toward change or concern for its impact on what we have already achieved permeate the field. They are found when we consider expanding the range of what art we teach and those taught. Some of us think of art education in this country as primarily concerned with school arts and preparing teachers, consultants, and teacher-education faculty. Along with this, there are long-standing programs of art for the mentally and physically handicapped, the elderly, kindergarten and preschool children, and the incarcerated. But there has been strong disagreement in the field whether these specialties should be included.

On the other side of this dichotomy art educators have been expanding our field even more. Some prepare teachers and arts administrators for non-public school sites such as museums, community arts and parks and recreation centers, urban rehabilitation facilities for substance-abuse victims, the homeless and adolescents. One university art education department has a new graduate program in consort with a school of business that expands art judgment into the market place as adults learn to manage and design the presentation of computerized Information.

Some of us have felt that art education should be expanded to include critical study of design in the environment as an integral part of art education. The ability to use aesthetic criteria to create qualities and symbolize values in human environments is particularly crucial now that space and other resources are becoming so limited and are being shared by people of such diverse backgrounds.

Many feel that the impact of television is so pervasive that ability to evaluate its influence must be developed in school. They see this as a critical communication skill needed by all students and best provided by studying art, design, art and television criticism, in addition to social criticism to adequately evaluate its messages. These trends indicate that both the content and the range of our field are expanding.

Controversy over the role of Discipline-Based Art Education (DBAE) continues. DBAE's main emphasis has been on elementary school art and not the field as a whole. This recognition should make it appear less threatening to some and less all encompassing to others. In terms of our analysis in Dichotomy 1. (fine art and the art of all the other people), DBAE contributes a highly developed use of Western art foundations and certain participants make some effort toward incorporating multicultural and women's art. It works across the spectrum from theory to practice and to teachers and administrators, using its subcultural view of art education.

Our concern here is with the whole of art education and whether it should be expanding in content and in populations served. It is difficult for me not to be polarized in answering this question but, fortunately for my main thesis my concerns go in both directions. In the expansive position, schools and schooling become more integrated with society generally. Some art educators are reaching out into the community to provide lifelong learning to the public and to people with specific needs for art. This helps art become better recognized as it is—an integral part of society. At the same time I believe strongly that we must not neglect our original purpose—to promote the use of art as a content area and learning tool in public school education. There are two particular reasons for this at this time.

First, we are living in an age where the visually descriptive image is becoming dominant over the written or spoken word. People need critical skills in decoding the use of design to affect imagery and the use of associational images to influence decisions and emotions. As a tool of politics, design can manipulate logical information with distorted meanings. A democratic society depends on educated citizens to make critical choices. People's dependence on television to judge the character and ability of candidates and compare issues requires that they learn how design and images are used to influence choice. We have always agreed that being able to read was a basic necessity for fulfilling the role of citizen. While we deplore the illiteracy that continues in this country it is even more deplorable that people who can read can still be manipulated without their knowing it, because they do not comprehend the language of visual information and the ways symbols and design can be used to distort information.

Second is the revitalization of our schools after years of neglect and social change. The world needs our continuing example of democracy in action, as more countries begin to practice it. The quality of our preparation of citizens is crucial. The question is: "How can we continue to be exemplary when we are falling behind in that basic ingredient that makes democracy possible— education in the humanities including broad-based visual arts, in addition to the social and physical sciences?" The ability to make qualitative decisions about the public and shared environment, and to critique political and other visual persuasions is crucial for citizens in this age of multicultural democracy in America.

Again, both ends of the "expand or maintain" dichotomy are needed, and they become continua between points that define the structure of art education. Neither one is right and the other wrong. Both positions are needed to maintain our functions in education and society.

137

Dichotomy 4. Melting-Pot or Multicultural Art Education

I focused on one segment of this dichotomy in another paper today, but it is also central here. Do we continue teaching art as if we had achieved one culture, or do we recognize change and diversity? Do we assume that we have achieved the melting-pot ideal, that all our minority groups have been assimilated into society and have had equal access to learning in our schools? Or do we recognize that the melting-pot ideal has been achieved only partially and selectively. Large percentages of students, particularly in urban areas, are living with other cultural realities than those of the school. Other children arriving from much of the world further increase the numbers whose culturally learned responses to art are different from those in school art programs.

There are extraordinary art teachers in the field who are gifted and knowledgeable in making aspects of the art experience vital to many diverse students. There are many in teacher education and social theory who try to enculturate students with awareness of other people's art. But schools are carriers of the dominant culture's middle-class, white value system and social organization. Adhering to the dominant culture is probably the main motivation for achievement by most teachers and administrators, irrespective of their cultural background.

Again, I am not asking that the dominant culture be rejected, although it does need change. It embodies much of our national identity, and in some ways we need a return to some of its central values such as integrity and the rights and worth of all individuals. But it can no longer be seen as the only culture that is operating in our society. More freedom of culture may need to be recognized just as we have valued freedom of religion.

To move toward a multicultural educational system is not an easy task for American political and educational bodies to undertake. Look how much resistance there has been to each effort of the women's movement to change culture and achieve full participation in the society, including the arts and academia. Being able to peer beyond one's own cultural system or accept change within one's culture takes study, experience, and openness. It is not easy to part with the conviction that one's own view of objective reality is the true one.

It has been hard for us to begin to assimilate the implications of change in Eastern Europe. Grasping what is changing in our own midst and the problems we have to solve here are difficult because we have not had the sudden challenges they face. Too many of us remain bound to what is familiar within our own cultural assumptions and limited experience, and avoid what is different. Others, overwhelmed by change and increasing diversity, question

138

if there is anything relevant art educators can do but preserve the ivory tower of art. But developing students' comprehension of multicultural art, developing awareness of their own cultural heritage in art and the ways art is used by cultures to express their values, attitudes, and sense of reality can strengthen intercultural communication and respect among people in a multicultural country. Our work in developing cross-cultural understanding through the images of art, and design—the grammar of visual imagery—helps meet this need and makes art education even more essential and central to education.

Dichotomy 5. Fine Art and School Art Versus Commercial Art

This is an old argument that as far as I know hasn't been addressed in a long time. The word, "commercial" may not be relevant any more. But the remnants of the dialogue continue. Fine artists and those most concerned with aesthetics in handcraft are most often selected as role models for school art. Those who design useful handcrafted or manufactured objects, or graphic and visual information, are generally considered to have lesser value. Fine art and school art, as a variation of fine art, continue to have the upper hand. There has not been a pressure group within NAEA to further the work of commercial art teachers in a long time. But the changing society, the dominance of television and computer-based communication in the daily lives of most of our population, and the fast developing emergence of computer-assisted fine art and computer graphics, as well as product and environmental design, may be forcing us to rethink old stereotypes that underlie the dichotomy. Certainly the new developments blur the concept of what we once called "commercial."

Production of work at both the fine and commercial polarities of art includes similar abilities, such as using culturally developed forms of aesthetics and design, improvising visual symbols, and creative problem solving. These traditions have histories, have evolved over time, and each has, if somewhat different, an art subculture and value-sharing supporters.

We also have to consider the social role of mass media as commercial art and its significance in education. Media-generated images project values that increase people's desire to buy. They load products with power to communicate, by amplifying and reinforcing their meaning through design and association with images of other desired things. The need to acquire is generated by images that suggest higher status, enhanced roles, more stimulating relationships, and excitement. Not only are products made important as things

139

we need to have, but that need and its meaning in our lives is projected as if it were our own cultural value system.

We have encouraged tolerance and understanding of differences in cultural background from cultures developed in community interaction evolving over long periods of time. But I think we need to take a long look at commercially manufactured, synthetic culture produced by a few opinion makers in brief periods of time. Most cultures develop by giving cohesion and pattern to the lives of people living in a group. Commercially generated culture is made to serve the needs of the economy by inducing individuals and groups to develop needs that support this purpose. It uses visual imagery to distort meaning for people who do not comprehend its methods. I suggest that as art educators we have an obligation to educate children to critique these messages and to have confidence in their own ability to make judgments about their own values and needs.

Ideally, art programs should include a core of study of the impact of art on the quality and meaning of life, including fine, crafted, ethnic, folk, popular, graphic, computer-based, environmental, and product design for personal and public spaces, costume, ornamentation, and celebration, and lastly, television. History, design, criticism, and cross-cultural analysis of these impacts can begin in elementary school and develop through general education courses in college and the community.

If art is presented as a vast phenomenon already touching everyone, then students could recognize it as something familiar and have a basis for extending their knowledge. They can start with what is familiar and branch out to using more critical and analytical skills. Gradually they can learn to compare the cultural and aesthetic meaning and impact of other aspects of art. Hopefully this will lead to three main goals—helping them to become more critical in their response to visual images, to develop sensitivity to quality in many art forms, and to become more multicultural in their responses to art.

Dichotomy 6. Theory and Research Versus Practice

There has been a long and persistent division in orientation in our field between those who theorize in higher education and those who practice in schools or communities. Concern by theorists for the what, why, and how of art education appears to have less value to classroom teachers overwhelmed with the day to day task of following school directives and managing the moment-by-moment interaction of kids with instruction.

Art methods and materials classes still are offered as the main and often only art course for elementary teachers. Often they reduce the anxiety of using unfamiliar art materials with children. But these classes seldom help teachers understand the contributions art education theory and research can give their teaching. The immensity of the task of reaching diverse students and exposing them to the myriad affects of art on their lives requires far more preparation and content than most of them appear to receive.

A root problem is that program and certification planners have little conception of what art education is all about and the time elementary teachers need to develop their own critical awareness of visual design and learn the fundamentals of teaching art in multicultural classrooms. We must remove the frill stereotype and identify art as a central communication system, which requires a background in implications from research and theory as well as curriculum and instruction in art.

Secondary art majors usually receive more work in art education than elementary majors. But they also need to comprehend art more extensively than their individualized studio-based art preparation gives them. Their future students will need to be considered from broad, individual, and socio-cultural perspectives. Not only do high school students face personal transitions, but they are moving from pre- to post-adolescent social environments that are themselves in bewildering states of sociocultural flux. They have had more years of indoctrination in TV culture. More of them than ever before were born in other societies. More of them come from divided families. More of them are poor, and poorer than their parents were as children. These conditions require much more background in foundations and art education social theory in secondary teacher education.

We also have the problem of finding art educators who have the range of interests, skill, and knowledge in both art and education, the sociocultural awareness, the broad general education, and who can keep abreast of ongoing changes in the day-to-day functioning of schools and the nature of school populations. When we find such teachers, we ought to recognize that their particular synthesis between theory and practice is a capstone to our success as a field. Reports of this synthesis need to be accepted as forms of publishable research and supported by other faculty who have the luxury of doing research in their more singular specializations. Art education administrators need to give special attention to such faculty to enable them to succeed in tenure track positions.

141

There is another aspect of this dichotomy that I have watched develop over the years. I was on the NAEA Board in the 1960s when job-alike divisions were made in the organization. This separated people who study the schools from those who practice in them. Now new sections develop that continue to divide the field into specializations. This is necessary to develop each area, but the interconnections need to be nurtured. There is some cross-fertilization in our journals for classroom teachers and where research is done in or about classroom learning and socializing processes. More work has been done on the interaction of art and society. But actual interface between people in theory and people in practice still is lacking in art education and in this professional organization. While extensive work has been done in curriculum development, over the past years, the synthesis needed now between broad-based theory and research and curriculum is still underdeveloped.

Classroom teachers, school administrators, art education faculty, and supervisors need to bridge the gap between theory and practice, not only because the field is dysfunctional if they remain separate, but because it is necessary for effective teaching in contemporary school environments. One outcome may be more rigorous master's degree programs to help experienced teachers discover and use the implications of relevant research to help solve teaching-learning and cross-cultural problems they are already familiar with. Continued faculty involvement in classrooms is necessary because schools are changing so rapidly.

Dichotomy 7. Focused Versus Expansive Foundations

Now we will look at the supporting fields that keep coming up in this paper. The more focused view uses fewer foundations. It perceives art education as a self-sufficient field and works to develop its own inquiry methods that are most appropriate for an effective field in education. It builds a conceptual framework for teaching about art and studio practice. It draws on art history and criticism in developing art concepts, studio traditions and inventions for art practices, and educational foundations in curriculum and instruction for developing programs.

The expansive viewpoint is more interdisciplinary. It includes broadly based concepts of art, more schooling beyond the classroom, and considers art's usefulness to learners from many backgrounds. It depends on information derived from more foundational fields—fields that contribute to knowledge about art education—and it uses different inquiry methods as appropriate.

A foundational area as defined here is a discipline or a field that underpins the development of another field. It can increase knowledge of the thought processes, ideas, practices, behaviors and relationships in operation in another field. As a field changes, so does its use of foundations. We will now look at each of our dichotomies to see what foundational fields may be relevant and what more are suggested as we bridge the gap between the two points of view.

Dichotomy 1, focused on the differences between teaching Western fine art and all the other people's art. If you, as an art educator, teach the art history, criticism, and aesthetics of Western fine art, you would draw on those fields or include them in your course requirements. If you teach studio in this tradition, you need such art foundations as painting, drawing and composition, sculpture, and printmaking. If you stay in the Western tradition but have moved into photography or computer graphics as fine art, you need foundation work in photography or computer science. If you are engrossed in teaching the other people's art, you could draw on background work in the established academic fields of folk art, popular arts, art in anthropology, and television criticism, for example. If you are bridging the gap between the two dichotomous positions and want to include all these arts, then your education should include some work in many of these foundations and their application to art teaching.

In *Dichotomy 2*, the art or the education of art education, the foundations you choose would depend on which position you take on the sub-dichotomies previously described. If your concept of art is Western fine art, the foundations just discussed would be appropriate. But if you are teaching crafts, product design, or advertising, then areas such as advertising psychology, ceramic engineering, or some work in interior architecture theory and design might be applicable. But if you also emphasize the education of art education, then current work in the social, cultural, psychological, historical, and philosophical foundations of education and our own literature are needed in the education of teachers and graduate students.

Dichotomy 3, concerns expanding or maintaining our field. A broad-based general education and a willingness to keep abreast of cultural change and social needs should help us make wiser decisions. We need much more study of the interface between art and human experience to identify where expansion is needed and a study of cross-cultural design to identify what is common and what is particular among cultures. Such studies could be made by teams of faculty and doctoral students with backgrounds in design and the social foundations of art education.

Dichotomy 4, asks whether we choose a melting-pot or a multicultural theory of education. In either case we need to draw on the social sciences and experience in multicultural classrooms to make our decision. Particularly, we need input from current demographics and political science as well as from educators who are specializing in changes in school populations. My interpretation is that we are far more a multicultural than a melting-pot society, and moving further in that direction. In an April 1990 televised interview, the Chancellor of The University of California reported that 50 percent of the students on the Berkeley campus are from minority backgrounds, but that the percentage in the freshman class is even higher. This indicates that this change is increasing and in a wide spectrum of society, and not just in less-advantaged urban centers.

Dichotomy 5, fine art and school art versus commercial art, is also set in a social context. Our decisions here depend on the breadth of our art experience, the subcultures of art we value, and the degree we reflect on the broad interface of art and humankind. It also depends on the breadth of our study and concern for the whole spectrum of society and its degrees of change.

The foundations needed to teach the broader concept of art change over time, and new ones develop. As mentioned before, a cross-cultural study of design needs to be made, not only to teach design to children from many cultures but to help children comprehend that the sorting and organizing of visual information happens no matter what art is being projected. If the environmental design and adornment arts are taught, foundation work in the history and practice of design in multiple cultures is needed by teachers. Some exposure by teachers to the literature in journalism and advertising is needed by those who prepare students to enter these fields and/or to critique them. There is not time here to explore all the foundations that might be useful, but it is a process that needs continual review.

Dichotomy 6, concerns people who work in theory and research versus teachers practicing in and out of public schools. There are foundations on each side of this question that need to be understood by both groups. Individuals have different needs to broaden their perspectives. People in theory and research can be at any point, from knowing a great deal about actual current classroom dynamics in a wide variety of cultural contexts to being much removed from them, but still doing valuable work. Classroom teachers, whether elementary art teachers, regular teachers, or middle-school and high-school art teachers can have broad concepts about art and be restrictive in education or be broadly based in education and have very limited views of art.

But to break down the conflict between the two, both faculty and teachers need enough background in their undergraduate work so stereotypes about one or the other activity are less apt to develop. Teacher training that addresses this problem gives students an appreciation of research and how careful generalizations can be made that apply to real situations in practice. As we have stressed before, researchers or interpreters of research for teachers are obligated to be knowledgeable about current classroom dynamics to be able to relate their work to them.

Dichotomy 7, summarizes some of the foundations that support these positions. As stated before, there is a pattern to the use of foundations. Narrowly focused dichotomous positions use fewer foundations than the more expansive. But as soon as we try to bridge the gap between these divergent views by setting them in a social context, we start adding more foundation areas to support them.

It is important to note that we have not covered opposing views in the philosophical and aesthetic domains. Nor has the question of child development focused on art as a singular behavior or on art as including the many facets of perception, cognition, creativity, information processing, field orientation, culture-patterned behaviors, or differences in personality. Dichotomies in these areas are as important as the ones selected but do not have the current is attention that their importance deserves. Other people working with this model would surely add other dichotomies to this list.

Some Final Reflections and Summary

In this paper I have looked at some of the dichotomous positions that divide us, set them in a larger social context to find the relationships between them and, from this perspective, identified their contributions to art education. From this position, art education can be seen as (a) including fine and all the other people's art, using hands-on in addition to learning-about activity, (b) encompassing both the art and education of art education and their supporting areas, (c) expanding programs for the public and increasing the breadth and cultural relevance of public school art, (d) moving beyond the melting-pot into multicultural reality, (e) reevaluating the stigma of commercialism, and teaching criticism, visual imagery, and design in mass communication and production arts, (f) developing more interaction between people in theory and practice, and (g) extending the use of the foundations in aspects of the social and behavioral sciences, studio art technologies, computer science, new developments in art history, criticism, and aesthetics and cross-cultural art and design with its impact on human experience.

Twenty-five years ago The Penn State Seminar established comprehensive foundations for our field. Specialists in each field reviewed the literature pertinent to art education—philosophy and aesthetics, the psychology of learning, the sociocultural backgrounds, the visual arts, and curriculum. Art educators who had specialized in relating these fields to art education gave parallel papers. This two-phase procedure was of particular importance in making transitions from the foundations to our field. The planners assumed that each area was necessary in order to identify individual and cultural differences to be utilized in developing curriculum in art. Unfortunately, much curriculum work has continued without following their lead. This is also true in some teacher education programs. But the foundations identified then are still central today. I believe we should update that seminar based on today's broad-based art and multicultural realities.

I would like to add a more personal note here. My writing over the last thirty years has focused on bridging the gap between research and practice. The text Rogena Degge and I wrote tried to provide continuity (based on the foundations of psychology and cultural anthropology) and flexibility (based on broad conceptions of visual art and design) for curriculum development and the practice of teaching children of differing aptitudes and cultures. Chapman and Feldman are among the few others who relate foundational areas to the realm of practice in their publications. But in terms of today's educational problems, we need many more people working on different aspects of the foundations and relating them to today's classroom populations.

This is a very complex profession—more than we have realized. It has room for people with many specializations and for people who can synthesize among the foundations. We need more interpreters who are current in areas of the supporting disciplines, who can apply them to art education theory, to teacher education, and to curriculum development in public school and outreach programs. We need specialists who are working in depth in singular aspects to build our knowledge base. We should give serious thought to restructuring our national organization and all its satellites and related organizations so that more cross-fertilization of ideas takes place. I urge that none of us be so immersed in our own point of view that we cannot network with the rest of the field.

Comprehensive analysis of the structure of our field should continue. We need to identify its nature more precisely in order to assess how well it relates to society's educational needs. Then we can achieve a more cohesive position from which to inform other educators, policy decision makers, and the public of our contributions. On the basis of this paper, I recommend that we identify our field as meeting the critical need for qualitative and analytical visual literacy in a dynamic, mass-media dependent multicultural democracy—a goal which can be obtained through comprehensive study of visual art and design.

References

Mattil, E. L. (1966). *A seminar in art education for research and curriculum development.* (Cooperative Research Project No. V-002). US Office of Education and The Pennsylvania State University.

McFee, J. K. & Degge, R. M. (1992). *Art, culture, and environment.* Dubuque: Kendall/Hunt.

McFee, J. K. (1990, April). Cultural diversity and change: Implications for art education. *Distinguished Fellows Symposium.* NAEA National Convention, Kansas City.

10

ART AND COMMUNITY: HISTORY OF THE INSTITUTE FOR COMMUNITY ART STUDIES

1965-1982

The Institute for Community Art Studies was established by a founding gift from Mrs. Lila A. Wallace in 1965 within the School of Architecture and Allied Arts, University of Oregon, as a research and public service organization concerned with public understanding and appreciation of art in a broad context. It was not established as an independent and self-sufficient unit, but rather to have the role of initiating, organizing, coordinating and contributing to community service projects that utilize the resources of the school along with other relevant resources in the University of Oregon. While the University provided funds for the basic maintenance of the Institute, the implementation of major projects "was" dependent upon outside resources. In addition to the founding grant, other funds for programs have been received from the Oregon Arts Commission; U.S. Office of Education; America the Beautiful Fund; John D. Rockefeller, III Fund; and through the Lane Intermediate Education District.

All of the Institute's endeavors, from its inception in 1966 to its conclusion in 1982, have involved study of the relations between communities and the arts, with the goal of nurturing and developing an engagement between the two. Central to the Institute's approach is a definition of the arts which includes environmental design; so that many of the Institute's efforts have sought to retrieve this aspect of the arts from its previous obscurity and neglect.

Among the many projects undertaken by the Institute in its sixteen year existence, three stand out as particularly extensive, the "Community Arts Study Program," which ran through the years 1966 to 1968, was perhaps the largest and most complex of all the Institute's ventures; the sponsorship of the two year sequence of Community Art Center Conferences in 1967 and 1968 was another major enterprise; and the ambitious "Program for Improvement of Art Education in Elementary Schools of Lane County," which ran from 1970 to 1974, achieved impressive results in this time.

The "Community Arts Study Program" was actually a series of related projects. It included an initial conference in 1966, entitled "Oregon Communities: Visual Quality and Economic Growth;" a set of four regional town meetings held in Newport, Pendleton, Coos Bay, and Klamath Falls in November, 1967; the very extensive work of the "Three Communities Study" which ran throughout 1968 in Albany. Newport and Bend; and, finally, in October 1968, the conference entitled "The Quality of Oregon Community Growth" which presented a summary of the results of the "Three Communities Study."

Community leaders from twenty Oregon cities attended the opening conference at Village Green to hear lectures and panel discussions, and to participate in discussion groups. The purpose of this conference was

"...to involve more people in decisions affecting a community's visual quality,

...to provide more criteria for evaluating decisions,

...and, to relate public school art to local and statewide problems.

These were done to:

...encourage the unique identity of Oregon communities as population and traffic increase, and standardization of buildings and highways foster uniformity;

...improve the quality of people's daily experience as they go out, between and through houses, buildings, streets and open areas of their communities;

...and, encourage sensitive, long-range planning as people react to the forces of change, improving rather than destroying the visual spirit or quality of their communities."

The Three Communities Project was an "in depth study of visual quality in three Oregon communities by ICAS staff and Art Education along with staff and students from the departments of Architecture, Landscape Architecture and Urban planning". The final report on the Study was issued in March 1969 with the title *Community Arts Study Program*. The purposes of the study as summarized in this report are:

"...to explore ways in which the professional staff and students of a School of Architecture and Allied Arts could work with townspeople. high school art teachers. and teenagers-in studying the functions, conditions and changes in their communities as a basis for making more qualified judgments about the quality of their environment."

"...to encourage community awareness of environmental design problems through an experimental course with art education and architecture consultants."

"...to provide people with more alternatives for making independent qualified decisions in relationship to the unique cultural, structural and geographic condition of their community."

"It was intended that high-school art teachers and students would be involved with townspeople in studying their communities. It was intended that interaction of professionals and townspeople would produce more workable curricular materials to be used for future study of communities for high schools and townspeople alike.

The outcomes worked toward were the development of meaningful and effective methods of involving adults and adolescents with environmental decision. It was hoped that the encouragement of art teacher participation in community design problems would lead to more effective and directly applicable design education in the schools; more cooperation between schools and community and more student concern for their communities."

The background for this effort is described in these terms:

"Problems of community renewal are often solved mainly by using economic and expediency criteria rather than concern for the visual and functional needs of the area or involving persons who have these concerns. As population increases, the need for an aesthetically literate citizenry to control and enhance the growth of towns and cities becomes crucial. General education in art in secondary schools traditionally has been more concerned with creating "art" rather than the development of working criteria for evaluating art and the visual environment."

This emphasis has not given future citizens the critical language nor reasoning understanding of environmental design problems so that they could state the case for better design in competition with the so-called 'hard facts' of economic considerations.

To encourage the development of environmental design as well as introducing it as a professional concern of the art teachers, there is need for both systematic curriculum development as well as cooperation with adults who are concerned with community design problems.

The program is based on the assumption that in a democracy everyone is responsible for what he contributes to the public view.

... Study of environmental design needs to be carried out in all communities and among all the students preparing to participate in American Society."

The major objectives of this study were stated as:

"1) to give participants working criteria and qualitative concepts through the rational study of design and environmental design problems as related to the history, developing trends, and culture of their community,

2) to involve high school art teachers in community design problems as a means of encouraging this activity in their work with students,

3) to explore and evaluate curricula for meeting this need."

The three towns selected for study—Bend, Albany and Newport—each represented "a distinct geographical area, with a unique historical development, land use and economic activity base." Bend (pop. 13,200) was a "high plateau winter sports, ranch trading center town." Albany (pop. 16,500) with its related towns of Scio (pop. 468), Lebanon (pop. 6,300), and Halsey (pop. 450) was a "river valley farming and industrial area." And Newport (pop. 5,750) was "a coast resort and commercial fishing center."

The types of program followed in each town were different in response to the different resources and needs of each location. In Newport, "Townspeople, school personnel and teenagers studied the community with professional staff help. Their findings were reported to the town via television and town meetings." The principal consulting staff in Newport were William H. Havens, Assistant Professor, Landscape Architecture, and Earl Moursund, Associate Professor, Architecture. Local coordinators were Robert Updenkelder, Marian Stovall and Elaine Shaeffer.

Happily, the Three Communities Program in Newport coincided with another ICAS program, the Newport Summer Study. In this project, which was supported by the America the Beautiful Fund, four graduate architecture and arts students conducted summer studies in Newport. Under the direction of Earl Moursund they looked at "four key aspects of the town's problems: 1) retired people's attitudes toward their living environment, 2) the usage and traffic problems of the harbor, 3) the relationships of the business district to the rest of the town, and 4) a symbol for community identity." Both ICAS groups were able to benefit from this conjunction of effort.

In the Albany area, "seminars were held on ways to study towns, and townspeople who were interested were encouraged to develop study groups." The principal consultant for this area was Richard Smith, Associate

Professor, Architecture. Donald B. Driscoll, Architect and ICAS Research Assistant, worked as a principal consultant for the town of Lebanon.

In Bend, "Professional staff and university students studied the town and presented their findings to the townspeople." The principal consultant was William Kleinsasser, Associate Professor, Architecture; and local coordinators were Richard Dedlow and Michael Shannon.

Some of the evidenced outcomes of the study are summarized in the report as the following:

1) When teenagers are asked to study the town, and their findings are listened to by teachers and by the civic leaders of the town, constructive ideas and projects can be developed so that young people can identify with their town, look at it objectively, and be active participants in community development.

2) Teachers can become more active citizens and become better able to help students understand their environment through these types of study.

3) Although our evidence is impressionistic, we did seem to see a change in town-school relationships in those towns in which all three groups of people had an opportunity to act together.

4) By analysis of professional-lay interaction in studying towns, a basis can be found for adult and high school curriculum materials, overcoming problems of professional language and sharpening specific key problems and their relationships to other variables which must be considered in environmental problem solving.

The conference—"Quality of Oregon Community Growth"—held in October, 1968, provided an opportunity to report on the coordinated activities of townspeople in Newport, Albany, and Bend with ICAS staff, and to share the insights gained with representatives from many other Oregon communities. About 60 persons attended the two-day session. The proceedings of this conference are included in the final report of the Community Arts Study Program.

Also included as an appendix in this report is the "Handbook for Community Study" developed by ICAS Research Associate, Donald Driscoll. This handbook ["a self-study guide that can be used with a minimum of professional assistance"] is intended for the use of "community organizations interested in studying the visual quality of their environment."

In the same years as the "Community Arts Study Program," the Institute sponsored a second major program—the 1967/68 sequence of Community Art Center Conferences. Both conferences were coordinated by ICAS member Gordon Kensler. In July 1967, ICAS, working in cooperation with the

Friends of the Museum of Art, Statewide Services of the Museum of Art and the Oregon Arts Commission, "brought together for the first time leaders from over 30 art organizations throughout the state. The central focus of the conference was to help the organizations provide more effective community service. Along with information and ideas on organizational problems, available resources, and examples of successful problems, the conference provided a setting for fruitful interchanges of ideas among the representatives from the organizations."

"During the summer of 1968, a follow-up Community Art Center Conference was held on the campus. The general focus was similar to the first one but with different topics that included reports from organizations on accomplishments that had been made during the year as a result of the previous conference." In the period following the conference, the Institute "maintained informal communication with many of the organizations and ... supplied information and speakers when requested."

Transcripts of lectures and discussions from both these conferences are available in the University of Oregon archives.

A third major ICAS undertaking—the "Program for the Improvement of Art Education in Elementary Schools in Lane County" ran from 1970 to 1974. As its name indicates, the program was established to design and implement an art curriculum for Lane County elementary teachers. As has been typical of the ICAS approach in many instances, the organization of the program emphasizes coordination with regional institutions and utilization of existing resources. Thus, in setting up the curriculum development project, the Institute worked in direct cooperation with the Lane Intermediate District. A major strength of the program derived its use of elementary personnel on the planning team. Eight educators from the county schools (teachers, principals and art coordinators) in conjunction with two intern-consultants and staff from the ICAS were involved in the initial planning. The program also engaged the P.T.A., the Eugene Junior League, the Maude Kerns Art Center, the Oregon Museum of Art, and the Oregon Arts Commission. In addition to the involvement of this regional network, the project was supported by a grant from the JDR III Fund.

Working with the assistance of all these groups, the Institute was able to issue an art education handbook for the intermediate grades, entitled *Art in the World Around Us*. As indicated by the book's title, the curriculum outlined in the book emphasizes problems of environmental design. The following statement of the "objectives of art education as developed by this program" is taken from the 1970/71 *Report on the Art In the Schools Project in Lane County, Oregon*:

1. Awareness of the distinct forms of art that man creates in his environment; expressions of man's feelings and ideas; signs and symbols; his
   use of objects; places to live, work, plan and objects to use.
2. Investigation of forms, sizes, shapes and colors as they change in space,
   viewpoint and light. (We live in a world which changes as we look at
   it; as it changes, our responses to it also change.)
3. Discrimination of the visual and functional properties of shapes, patterns, lines, colors, textures, structures and spaces. (Careful observation is necessary if we are to become fully aware of the variety of
   shapes and forms in the world around us.)
4. Recognition of the visual and functional relationships among objects,
   concepts and qualities. (We can try to see how certain things or ideas
   may be grouped because of features which they have in common.)
5. Exploration of the potentials of tools and materials and the development of ease in using them to express ideas and solve problems. (By
   using various tools in various ways we can discover how each can help
   us handle our chosen materials most effectively to serve our purposes.)
6. Development of one's own individuality through invention, innovation,
   reorganization and improvisation. (One of the things that art work
   shows us repeatedly is that no two people "see" or create in exactly the
   same way. To gain a sense of our "specialness" is one of the most
   important things that we can learn through art.)
7. Development of a language for talking and thinking about art. (Like
   science, geography or any other area of study, art uses terms that are
   designed to give us a common ground for understanding each other.)
8. Development of critical and evaluative powers. (Part of learning
   through art is done by looking carefully at art works and giving considered judgments on their qualities.)
9. Seeing how men express their differing values through the way things
   are put together and arranged. (Through the design of dress, architecture, jewelry, cities, sculpture and film making, the value of things is
   expressed.)
10. Development of sensitivity to natural forms, as they function in nature
    and are modified by man; understanding the aesthetic and functional
    properties of natural forms, trees, plants and land forms as changed by
    nature and man.

In acknowledging the relationships between visual and "economic, political, structural, spatial and social factors" in environmental design issues, the
curriculum has the potential to be integrated with other school subjects, especially social studies.

However, those involved with this curriculum development program were concerned to achieve more than the construction of a theoretical base. An essential feature of the program was the use of workshops about the curriculum as a means of working towards the actual implementation of the curriculum in the classroom. An initial day-long workshop for supervisors, principals, art organization representatives, and parents was offered to acquaint the educational community with the objectives of the art education program. And the publication of the handbook was complemented by, a series of workshops open to all elementary personnel in the district. These workshops were offered through the University of Oregon's Continuing Education Department, and typically lasted 10 weeks with three hours of class per week. In 1971, the first year of the workshops, more than 270 elementary teachers attended; by the end of the second year, 24% of all the elementary teachers in the district had taken the course.

In order to make the book as useful as possible for concrete classroom practice, participants were surveyed again after their return to the classroom. This review of the use of the curriculum in actual teaching situations was conducted by F. Graeme Chalmers, an Art Education doctoral student. The results functioned as important additional feedback in the continuing development and revision of the *Art in the World Around Us* curriculum.

In addition to developing the *Art in the World Around Us* handbook, the Art Education Improvement Program also worked to integrate the community's existing visual and performing art resources with the new curriculum. In cooperation with the Oregon Museum of Art, slides were made of outstanding works in the Museum for distribution to schools by the Instructional Media Center of the Lane IED. "The purpose was to use the slides as illustrative material in the curriculum to relate the ways artists use space, use formal and affective qualities in art, etc. Further, the students would be better prepared to respond to these works when they see them in actuality in the Museum."

The Institute also coordinated its curriculum efforts with the Junior League's "Art in the Schools" program. This program was operated in conjunction with the Maude Kerns Art Center; the center collected art works for exhibit, and the League provided display models and organized exhibits in the district schools.

In addition to these three clusters of major endeavor, the Institute also sponsored the Elementary Art Education Handbook, which was produced in cooperation with the Oregon Art Education Association and the Oregon Department of Education. Officially titled *Elementary Art Education: A Handbook for Oregon Teachers.* The handbook was an outgrowth of work done in 1975-76 when the Institute supported Bev Jones as an intern in the State Department of Education. The material she developed at that time for the art section of the *Basic Guide for Oregon Education* had to be substantially edited for ICAS interest in feedback and revision, every copy includes a questionnaire on user reactions. This handbook proved helpful in the initial development of a liaison with the Eugene District 4J to work with their elementary program.

In 1974-75 the Institute sponsored a "study of responses of docents to art at Bush Barn, Salem, to identify ranges of affective and analytical responses."

In 1975 the Institute supported a research survey which collected information about the make-up of the NAEA membership. The questionnaire, developed by a University of Oregon graduate seminar led by Gordon Kensler and June McFee, was organized into five groups of questions: personal data, professional satisfaction, the school program, undergrad and graduate preparation, and professional organization involvement. The survey was sent to NAEA members in the Association's November 1975 Newsletter. The analysis of the response was primarily done by ICAS Research Assistant, Kristen Sweet; and the results were summarized in a 1977 paper entitled *The NAEA: A Sampling of our Identity*, by K. Sweet, B. Jones, G. Kensler, and J. McFee. (A copy of this paper is on file in the University of Oregon archives.) Perhaps one of the most exciting generalizations suggested by the data is that the typical (in 1975) art teacher found working with students the major source of satisfaction in their job.

In the years 1975 and 1976, the Institute sponsored a program to identify conceptual relationships between public school curricula and University of Oregon Museum collections. Institute Assistant, Dianna Kale interviewed 4J elementary curriculum coordinators in all subjects, reviewed the museum collections for linkages, and prepared materials for teachers and docents to make museum tours more meaningful for school students.

In the academic year 1975-76, the Institute aided Mary Christopherson in preparation of her in-depth study of the Sculptural Symposium; part of this report became her M.S. terminal project. Institute staff helped with research design and analysis, and the Institute also provided some materials and secretarial help. Ms. Christopherson worked as a part-time ICAS employee preparing tapes and transcripts of the Symposium for filing in the AAA Library.

In the same academic year, Institute personnel also provided help to Mildred Roske in her preparation of her dissertation on the history of values towards the American home. ICAS staff aided in research design, supplied resource materials, and reviewed the manuscript.

In 1978 the Institute "worked with District 4J Eugene Public Schools, with an exploratory program in the Crest Elementary School. Barbara Boyer was an intern working with the teachers in developing programs in art and visual perception, with June McFee as advisor." Ellen Kotz, Institute G.T.F. for this year, also participated in the planning and execution of this program. "Programs included:

1) helping teachers themselves become more visually aware

2) understanding of the social and aesthetic functions of art

3) developing concepts for thinking about art

4) developing strategies for helping students of different abilities respond to art

5) learning to use the Museum of Art more effectively with children."

At the end of the year District Coordinator, Dr. Martha Harris, described teacher response as very enthusiastic.

In this year Ellen Kotz also worked on a critical review of research reports at NAEA conferences. Several research proposals were worked on by Ellen Kotz in 1976-77; a proposal was submitted by ICMA to the National Trust for Historic Preservation to develop a secondary school curriculum on historic preservation decision-making.

ICAS Publications

Oregon Communities: Visual Quality and Economic Growth, 1968.

Community Art Studies Program, 1969. (Final Report, U. S. Office of Education Project No. 6-3054).

Art in the World Around Us: Guideline to Art in the Elementary School Grades Four, Five and Six (c. 1974). (In cooperation with Lane I.E.D., with support from the John D. Rockefeller, III Fund).

Elementary Art Education: A Handbook for Oregon Teachers, 1977.

ICAS also contributed to the publication of: *Survey of the Arts in Oregon*, 1967.

11

SOCIETY AND IDENTITY: A PERSONAL PERSPECTIVE

First Women's Caucus NAEA, Miami, 1975

Having been asked to address this group from my particular perspectives, I have had to do a lot of sorting in my own mind to try and select experiences that would be illustrative of problems that would be useful to you today.

What has appeared is a time line of social contexts which changed as society changed and my own responses to that context as pressures within myself and my own search for identity as a woman, as an artist, and later as an art educator came into conflict with society's role expectations. I am not talking about myself so much as about a woman in the interplay of psycho-social-cultural forces.

Before beginning, I must state two assumptions. One, that each of us is unique, each finding her own way through different aspects of the subcultures we experience, though there are similarities in our experiences that are related. This is what makes a case study useful. There are things we can all learn from anyone's reflections on experience. Two, that I am not at all sure when resistance to what I was doing was due to the ideas that seemed important to me, or to the fact that I was a woman, or to some combination of the two. I assume I could have gotten away with iconoclastic ideas more as a man than as a women.

When we analyze our own experience and emerging self-concept, we need to be aware of the values and belief systems of the cultures we came from, the attitudes of the men and women in our families, and the dynamics produced by their likenesses and differences. The roles they play do influence children. I had some very non-typical females in my family who influenced my early sense of what a woman could be. Eighty-four years ago my widowed, paternal grandmother, driving herself and her young son in a horse-drawn wagon, was one of 20,000 people who raced into the Cherokee Strip of Oklahoma to claim land. She settled in a new town, built a sod hut, and set herself up as a dressmaker, one of the few roles open to her. She worked until she was over seventy. She was a powerful, independent, determined woman all her life. Also an aunt, as I remember, in the 20s sold creosote piling for building shipping facilities, wore knickerbockers, and drove a sports car at what appeared to me to be reckless speeds. But these women were different from those I met at school. In 1926, I remember vividly being grabbed by the shoulder by an irate teacher who told me I was not to play baseball with the boys but come up to the girls' playground and stay there. The frustration and hostility to society this one act produced was very strong; it is then that I became jealous of the freedom boys had, disliked what girls said and did, and developed a certain amount of self-hatred because I was female.

My mother was from the South and very much a displaced person in the still then pioneer culture of the Pacific Northwest. She very much wanted me to grow up to be a " lady," to learn social graces which she found missing in that area. But she had another side—she was a gifted musician and composer with a fiery Irish disposition—a veritable Martha Mitchell. Her way to resolve doing something in this world and do it in a lady-like way was in the arts. Since she had absolute pitch, I soon quit the violin and decided to be an artist—at age twelve. Mark Tobey and Morris Graves were the artists around which the art world of the Northwest grew. I studied with a member of this close group, Guy Anderson, who, during the worst of the depression, was very happy to give lessons to a scrawny, shy little girl whose mother was pushing her to be "something."

But inside the shyness other ideas were interesting me. I was obsessed with aviation—to learn to fly was my greatest goal. In the late 20s and early 30s women aviators were coming into their own. Amelia Earhart was my ideal. I studied airplane engines, drew plans, and read all I could get my hands on about those marvelous women who were fearless, skillful, and held up as important pioneers by society generally. During that period women were making tremendous progress. They were going into medicine, psychology, anthropology, and, of course, education. Ruth Benedict was one of the 22 women who got Ph.Ds in anthropology between 1910-1940—out of a total of 51 at Columbia, 43 percent were women! Films of the period pictured women as intelligent, competing with men in games of wit. Rosalind

Russell, for example, was often cast as the girl reporter who outsmarted the men around her. Romance always triumphed, but it was more a marriage of equals, an appreciation of personality, as well as sex.

It was, in many ways, a great time to become an adolescent as a girl, but I remember learning early that if you wanted to be popular and get taken to dances you had to keep your interests to yourself. You didn't talk about airplane engines, women flyers, or art to boys. Being popular was something my mother cared a great deal about and I was pushed into a social life that produced mixed feelings. To gain identity, to be someone, one had to play roles.

You weren't really a person whose inside and outside self was the same. Also, now I see the trap mothers were in, and still are in, to some degree. Mothers push their daughters to be popular and have dates so they can have a better pool from which to get a husband. This was the one dominant goal, not only for getting ahead, but for survival. Mothers of sons pushed them to succeed, not only to prove they were good mothers, as this was their means to enhance their own identity, but to gain status through their sons' accomplishments. This is what the counterculture threw in the face of parents. Kids were willing to gamble with their lives and their future to break this pattern. But now six, eight, ten years later, they are back in school trying to work their way back into a system that is itself groaning with adjustments.

During the 30's I distinctly remember resenting strongly I'd been born a woman. I remember how much I admired my father and, for a brief period in high school, wanted to be, like him, a lawyer. It was a great shock when he squelched that completely. No daughter of his would go into law. He'd send me to college but not to study law. He also told me it was a waste of time to take solid geometry or calculus, both of which I wanted to take in high school. What amazes me now is that I accepted his word as final.

This conflict of roles, between what was possible for women to be, and what most of that sub-culture of society I was exposed to considered appropriate roles for women, were indeed in conflict. None of the women among my family's friends worked. My mother assumed I would never work. Be an artist—yes—but never enter the working world. This was in conflict with the women in the family who did work. It was the push of upward mobility which in that era meant the women in an upper middle class family didn't work for money. Women were symbols of status—not beings with independent ambitions. Talents were to be used for worthy causes where one could contribute her efforts in things that added status, but one got status mainly from what the man in the family did.

During my college years I studied art in Chicago with Alexander Archipenko. He was a man who had great respect for women and their intellect. His wife was a brilliant woman. His sculptures of women always had tremendous dignity—a search for the essence of being. He gave me much encouragement and confidence. Never there or at the University of Washington art department when I graduated did I find any experience of discouragement as a woman in art. Opportunities to exhibit in competitive shows and the W.P.A. support for the arts at that time provided many avenues for seeing one's work among that of other artists. There were quite a few women exhibitors.

That era of the 20s and 30s came to an end in 1941 when World War II started. Women were encouraged for that short period to do things they had not done before in non-combat service—flying transport planes, manning alert stations, building ships and planes. My own brief time in the service taught me how isolated my life had been from much of society. It was in an Army hospital that I came to grips with the shallowness of much of what I had been taught was important. After the illness, I was discharged and finally entered the working world, following my husband in airforce training, from camp to camp doing whatever work I could find. It was almost the most important part of my education. I learned much about class stratification and what it was like to be a working girl, behind the counter. I met and learned to appreciate a much wider variety of people. For the first time I saw a woman who had been beaten to a pulp by her husband but who wouldn't prosecute him because he was her husband.

Then the war was over, and the return of women to traditional roles began in the late 40s and 50s. Big families became the vogue, with the post-war baby boom. The acquisition of material goods after the rationing of the war years began to accelerate. A great fear of being different or not acceptable spread through the McCarthy era. My husband and I settled down to raise a family, and I attempted to keep painting, but I couldn't fit the role of housewife and aspiring socialite which was expected of me. Soon I started an art department in the local community college and commuted to a state college to get a master's degree. I clearly remember a close family friend who was also chairman of the board of the college cautioning me, "You aren't going to be a career woman, with a husband and a baby, are you?" I assured him I was. My students at the community college had a show in the main hotel, but we found them covered with butcher paper as the modern art was offensive to patrons. A battle over whether modern art should be taught in the college ensued, and my contract was not renewed to teach.

Fortunately, my husband was as dissatisfied with business as I was with living in the constraints of a conservative town of 50,000 people. As one of our old friends from the town said, we were the first straight people in town to start a counter-culture movement. So in 1954 we sold our home and his business and started over again.

I entered the School of Education at Stanford and he picked up his undergraduate work.

Competition for grades was acute. I clearly remember remarks like, "Why are you working so hard? You'll never use it. I don't approve of your being in this program." At graduation, the man sitting next to me said that his superior would not approve of me. A professor agreed it was all right in music and art, but not in social foundations or philosophy. My advisor in art education tried to discourage me the first day, saying they really didn't have a program, why didn't I go back home.

But there were people—both men and women—who were encouraging. But if it hadn't been for one woman, Dr. Pauline Sears, who helped me accept myself as a woman as well as sharpen my intellectual skills, I would never have gotten my degree. She was a model of a professional person of national stature, who had raised two children and was the wife of another well-known psychologist.

Upon graduation, the art department hired me to teach elementary education courses and supervise secondary school teachers—a task many men at that time did not like to do. I was hired as an instructor with my doctorate for $4,800. But there were people in the doctoral program who needed help, so I developed graduate course work as an overload. During the next five years with new people coming in, the Stanford Perceptual Studies in art education developed. I am very proud of those five years and the people who graduated. Most of them are very well known in art education today.

My leaving Stanford as I did would never have happened today. At that time there were very few women staff members, and they were under-promoted and under-paid. There was a policy of not hiring their own graduates, male or female. However, the College of Education unanimously voted to have me transferred to that college and for promotion to associate professor. But my immediate superior in the art department disagreed vehemently with what I was doing in art education and was in a position to veto my promotion. In this case, conflicts over ideas were an important factor. But I do believe that if I had been a man, two things would have happened: one, the conflict of evidence would have been considered more by the university; and two, I would have fought back, as I certainly would today. My students did all they could, but it was before the days of activist protest.

163

At that point my husband was finishing his Ph.D. in anthropology and was appointed to the staff at the University of Arizona. I was called by the dean of the College of Education the same weekend and offered a position. We arrived in the fall with my appointment not completed, and it never was. The president of the University refused to sign it for nepotism policies—a policy that mainly affected women. There were 15 Ph.D.s and one M.D. in Tucson at that time who were unemployed because their husbands were on the staff.

During the three years in Arizona I was able to keep up professionally as visiting lecturer working around the country, teaching part time at Arizona State University and establishing the doctoral program there. We tried to establish a research institute but could not get private foundation or government funding. Who ever heard of a research institute made up of females? At the end of this period was the Penn State Seminar which of course was a landmark in art education. Preparing for that was a saving grace for me professionally and in terms of my own sense of purpose.

In early 1965, the president of the University of Oregon was Arthur Flemming, formerly head of H.E.W. He was a man who was ahead of his time. He wanted more women on the faculty. When money became available to establish a University-based Community Arts Studies Institute, I was hired to develop it. I was also promised I could start a doctoral program in art education.

There was considerable resistance to my coming.

A delegation came and asked me to give back the grant for the Institute, promised me I would never get the doctoral program off the ground, and that the University should never have hired me. I also overheard at a cocktail party that I was just a housewife the University hired because they wanted the money from the grant.

But that was also 1965, and things were beginning to shift in the national scene. Resistance to a doctoral program faded into more apparent issues, and we have been building it ever since with the percentage of women in the program increasing every year.

All of you are very familiar with these last ten years. Opportunities for women have changed, but deep-seated attitudes learned through centuries of cultural conditioning are slow to change. We have gained in legal rights, but much remains to be done. We are changing our self-concepts but we are pioneering new domains and still finding our way. The uncertainties of the economy and resource projections ahead must not let us repeat the backward trend of the fifties and early sixties.

If you will bear with me, I would like to analyze what I see now as more subtly pervasive influences on women that may take longer to change.

One is that you are accepted as "one of the boys" in some academic contexts, not as an intellectual woman or person. You are a woman out of role—you get the "you think like a man" syndrome as if it were a compliment. No matter what your intellectual contribution, you are a lesser person if you don't measure up in some degree to the cultural stereotype. The danger is if you believe this. It is hard not to, when its truth is suggested to you so pervasively and consistently.

But the women's movement in many of its ramifications has been a rejection of this dualism. We are learning to respect each other as people, as professionals, and as scholars and artists; support each other and not believe the stereotypes about ourselves. What you younger women and the women's movement generally have done in these last ten years has given me a new freedom and sense of support I have not had before.

Now I would like to review briefly some psychological research about sex differences and then draw some generalizations about social effects from my own experience. The stereotype is that there are many kinds of valued men, unique, different, but there is only one ideal woman and all others are categorized as variations away from that norm. Those women who do vary from the norm too much, if they excel are thought of as manlike, and always a lesser man.

This is changing slowly, but I believe it is part of the resistance to the Equal Rights Amendment. There is a fear of having this many more dynamic individuals in society; that control of society would be lost; that change would come too fast.

I.K. and D.M. Broverman, *et al.,* in a penetrating study reported in the *Journal of Consulting and Clinical Psychology* 1970, Vol. 34, the effects of the depth of cultural conditioning. They asked 79 men and women clinical psychologists, psychiatrists, and social workers to write three descriptions of the ideally healthy person, the ideal healthy male, and the ideal healthy female—then an unhealthy person, unhealthy male, and unhealthy female. What they found was that the *unhealthy* person = an *unhealthy* male = a healthy female. The difference between the healthy female and the healthy person was that she was "less competitive, less aggressive, less objective, more submissive, more dependent, more easily influenced, ...more emotional, more conceited about her appearance, and more aversive to mathematics and science."[1] These were all professional people, supposedly less influenced by stereotyping, all conditioned by cultural values to stereotype people who are only these ways in the degree they accept cultural norms. What is frightening is that these people try to help people reach the cultural stereotype of mental health and not what may be appropriate for them as an individual person. I well remember the guilt I felt when a school psychologist told me I was much too ambitious for a woman.

Now this study was done in 1970, I posit that greater change has taken place from 1970-1975 than at any period prior to this. The biggest force for change is women's own changed self concepts and some increased opportunity to try their potentials in a broader range of activities. A woman no longer needs to feel she is abnormal in some degree because she has drives to be highly creative, independent, or intellectual, or to take leadership. This is the heavy weight we are losing. Let's consider more data.

All stereotypes are based on somewhat false assumptions. The assumption that men are more independent and intelligent than women is one of them. When individual differences are considered, half the women are more intelligent than half the men when variations due to social conditioning are eliminated. Crutchfield, who found the average scores for women on conformity measures to be higher than men in 1955, posits that a present retest would provide a change. But even in 1955, a large percent of women were less conforming than a large percent of men—so where do many women fit in that stereotype?[2]

Marjore Honzik of the University of California compared the same males' and females' I.Q. scores at age 18 and 40 in 1973 and another group at age 17 and 48. She found I.Q. scores had not gone down overtime and in some areas such as verbal skills were increasing. Interestingly enough, girls at ages 17 and 18 had a mean below boys but in their forties had a similar mean equal to men. Honzik reported that many of the forty-year-old women reported that they expected to do much more poorly than when they were in school—when their actual I.Q. mean had gone up. Their expectations were not in line with their ability to perform.[3]

I.Q. as you know, is not thought of now as a unitary trait, but appears to be a cluster of separate traits that develop at different rates and continue much longer than ever suspected, with some cases of gain beyond 80. There is considerable evidence that teenage and even thirty-year-old women's I.Q. scores are lower than at age 40. Which suggests either change in actual I.Q. or the influence of social expectations on women at the earlier ages that depress performance. But it is at these ages that life goals, treatment and encouragement by schools and parents are conditioned by test results.

From my own experience and from what I have studied, we see that our experience is an on-going system. We continuously are in a systematic interaction between our own growth and development as we are learning from our family, adult models, peers, and the larger society and the changes in ourselves and society. Our behavior at any given time is influenced by all these factors as they are changing. As women we can say we have a better climate for developing our potential now than ever before. We are developing a peer group society to whom we can give strength and an in-group society from whom we can gain strength; to be independent, intelligent, creative women, as men have had for centuries.

Our greatest need is to see ourselves and all people as people with far more potentials for development in far more different ways than our stereotypes would allow, The gentle, compassionate, sensitive, creative, intelligent male has suffered as much from stereotyping as many of us have. We need to find more ways to achieve mental health. We need broader definitions of mental health. To be full persons, we don't need to have the male goal as our goal—but as people, find what is our most natural way to define our individuality. What this means, of course, is a redefining of the nature of what society can be. It is the fear of this in ourselves and in society at large that keeps us back. But of all the single factors that could make world systems work more efficiently in this limited resource/space capsule we live on is to change the status of women world-wide. The birth rate decreases as the status of women increases. Drastic reduction in the birthrate worldwide would effect the projections on resource limitation in every dimension. Coupled with more intellectually and creatively productive women we could double our potential to solve our environmental and social problems. This may seem an unattainable dream, but more of us are dreaming, and out of such dreams come ideas, and with ideas the power to develop them.

I want to thank all of you who are so actively working on developing an awakened female consciousness. This can lead to a more humane human consciousness for all peoples of the world.

Notes

[1] K. Broverman, D. M. Broverman, et al., "Sex-Role Stereotypes and Clinical Judgments of Mental Health," *Journal of Consulting and Clinical Psychology, 1970, 34,* p. 1-7.

[2] R. S. Crutchfield, "Conformity and Character," *American Psychologist, 10* (1955) pp. 191-8.

[3]M. P. Honzik, "Predicting I.Q. Over the First Four Decades of the Life Span," Paper: Society for Research in Child Development, 1973.

12

CULTURAL, ENVIRONMENTAL AND INDIVIDUAL INFLUENCES ON PROFESSIONAL DEVELOPMENT

Historical Lecture Series¹—Achievement Award
School of Fine Arts, Miami University, 1981¹

As requested by Miami University's School of Fine Arts, the purpose of this paper is to identify the history of the people and events that have influenced and nurtured my work. I will focus mainly on the relationship of art to the individual and society, and the effects of environment and culture on the art that is created and how art is taught.

Childhood Environment and Culture

1917-1930

The physical environment and climate of my early years had a profound and lasting effect: Pacific Northwest rain forests, the inland sea, sounds of sea birds, surf and tug boats, the shroud of mist and fog moving through trees; the sweet-sour smell of woods and salt air. I had time and freedom to wander alone among tide pools, over piles of driftwood, through dense woods, along country roads, and was nurtured to savor the variety of nature in the changing light of days and the slow shift of seasons.

The intensity and tensions of a multi-cultural family included the pragmatism, discipline and futurism of the Western pioneer stock of my law trained father, and the displaced remnants of Southern social structure, passionate love of music, freedom and creativity of my mother and her deep study of metaphysics and idealism.

169

Elementary education was restrictive, dreary, and in an ugly school. Art was prescriptive. I clearly remember the boy who could cut out better wooden parrots and paint them most like the picture, who got the rewards while the rest of us suffered with our incompetence. I also remember the woman's washing that came out each Monday outside the 4th grade classroom. Even then I wondered what her life was like.

Art and Secondary Education

1930-1935

My junior high had a kindly principal and an art teacher who, though a traditionalist, introduced us to the mysteries of art and water colors. The neat boxes of paints in the store room were very impressive. One marvelous day it snowed, and she stopped being a teacher and became an artist; set up her easel at the window and captured the scene with her spellbound students all around. She kept it up for three days.

But outside of school I had painting lessons from a fine Northwest painter, Guy Anderson, who helped me translate in some small degree the effects of diffused light onto canvas. Since he was one of a group of artists, Kenneth Callahan, Mark Toby, Morris Groves, I was introduced to their work. When the Seattle Art Museum was built, many opportunities occurred to see the impact of Northwest environment on these artists. At fourteen I won a blue ribbon at the State Fair. This made art seem more important, because I had another interest; then women were flying. Engines intrigued me, and I poured over pictures of engines and tried to draw them as a means of capturing in some way the essence of the freedom of flight. An interest in science and technology was born. Also at that time my mother brought home a catalogue of an exhibit of French Impressionists from the DeYoung Museum in San Francisco. This one catalogue had a tremendous impact. I kept it for years.

A high school art teacher also helped focus my interest in art. An intense, no nonsense, rotund little woman whose round red earrings bobbed on thin chains as she bounced around the room. In a disciplined environment she encouraged individualized expression. Two other teachers also had an impact: the geometry teacher who quietly introduced us to mathematical form, which I found had beauty, and a geography teacher who stimulated our interest on all the diverse peoples and countries that circled the Pacific rim—Alaskan Indians to Australian Aborigines—Juneau, Alaska to Freemantle Western Australia, with Hawaii, Fiji, and New Hebrides in between.

170

Also a factor at this time was the arts brought to the Seattle area from these parts of the world found in Museums, galleries, and people's homes. Arts of Asia were predominant, but more important to me were the arts of the Northwest Coast Indians and Eskimos; totem poles, robes, carvings, jewelry were all there. These, too, were part of that climate and had been absorbed by these people centuries before. Contemporary artists were also affected by it. And there was a marvelous old shop on the waterfront that had artifacts from the Pacific Rim and magnificent Kwakiutl robes attached to the ceiling.

College and Art School

1935-1940

The first two years at Whitman College, a small liberal arts school, had broad educational value. Two teachers stand out today: Proceptus E. Costas, a Greek professor of Latin who instilled a love of history, the dissemination of ideas, as well as a love of the derivations of words and meanings from one language to another, and a class in physics by S. B. L. Penrose Jr., who wanted us to see the relationships of then known forces and vectors, and instilled a keen interest in the development of ideas in that field. This continues at a layperson's level today. An interest in systems and interrelations was developing, begun perhaps with my mother's involvement with music and metaphysics and reinforced by studying the interrelations of peoples around the Pacific.

A monumental change took place the summer at the end of my sophomore year. Alexander Archipenko came to teach art at the University of Washington. The first days were not much different than other classes. Students set up individual still lifes and drew and painted. Soft-spoken Archipenko, with his piercing deep-seated eyes, talked individually to students. He didn't seem to be paying any attention to me, but I finished a competent painting of a still life. Just at that time he came up behind me and said, "Don't ever paint like that again." It was one of the most freeing moments of my life. So much time had been spent learning to conform to the right way to paint, to get good grades, to belong to the right groups—to be a woman as then prescribed in upper middle class society. Here was a challenge by a man of great individual richness and international renown as a sculptor, turning me away from outside pressure to conform, to valuing my own responses. Though I didn't realize it then, what most came out was the effects of light on shape—childhood experience in rain forests. A painting done after class

171

was accepted for a Northwest Artists Juried Show and I began my life as an artist.

Archipenko encouraged my parents to let me go back to Chicago to study in his studio with a few other students. Suddenly I was in a totally new world, of galleries, The Chicago Art Institute, and the beginnings of the Chicago Bauhaus, all of which I had contact. I lived in a residence for women students in music, theatre, dance, and the visual arts. Archipenko demanded his students work from 8:30 to 4:30 each day, and have little social life. While he let me do some sculpting, he said I was a painter and I must paint and paint and paint. He introduced me to Katherine Kuh and I spent many late afternoons listening to the artists who gathered in the back room of her gallery on Michigan Boulevard. Artists from Mexico, Europe, as well as the United States, came. I absorbed what they said about art, but was naive of their reputations, as I didn't know enough of the art world to know their importance.

Suddenly, my family decided I must return and finish college and re-enter the social structure of pre-World War II college and sorority life. From this perspective, 44 years later, the socialization that made me leave that brief, marvelous experience in Chicago and do what one "should" do according to the mores of the time are almost unbelievable now. My family was impelled to keep their daughters in a position where they would marry in an acceptable social strata (though I doubt if they even consciously thought of it that way). What is even more appalling is that I accepted their direction. I report this because it is evidence of the counter socialization that affects women artists and women even today.

Fortunately, I kept on painting and exhibiting. At the University of Washington I studied aesthetics with Melvine Rader. Another very powerful art experience was studying with Amedee Ozenfont, the French purist, who was on campus. Studying with him was the antithesis of studying with Archipenko. He was a demanding technical perfectionist. One planned and executed *one* painting a quarter. Every stroke was pre-planned. One was a prisoner of one's prior design decisions. Innovation, serendipity, ongoing inspiration were not allowed, only refinement of structure and form after the first design was made.

The experience of working with these two powerful artists who had such different concepts of an artist's work and teaching was certainly one of the most profound influences on me as I became an educator. The *way* art is taught is surely as important as what is taught. The impact on the individual—and its long range and deep seated effects—were very clear. I carry the impact of that conflict yet today. But it has made me much more concerned for the individual student, and for the effect of differences in affective teaching. After I graduated, my father, in despair about my interests in marriage, sent me off to secretarial college so I could support myself. I left the college after exploding publicly to the director when he lectured us on being good fence sitters—do what our bosses said and never voice an opinion.

Fortunately for all concerned, I did meet and became engaged to a very intelligent, widely read and gentle young man, Malcolm McFee, who was trying to prepare himself for what his family saw as acceptable behavior— entering the world of business. With the prospects that my future was now secure, my father let me go on to Cornish School of Art in Seattle. Again, I was able to paint as long as I took courses in commercial art as well. These were excellently taught and the discipline, the design and drawing concepts and skills learned were important to my becoming an art educator.

The War and Post War Years

1941-1954

As I write this now, I am surprised that at 23 I had no idea of teaching—and I had never earned a penny. In 1941, just before we entered WWII, Mac and I were married and I accepted the role of a dependent housewife. I could not paint during that time. But another event contributed to my understanding of drawing. I was selected as one of a group of fine arts artists who were part of an experiment for the Boeing Company. They were trying to see if we could be trained in six months to be production illustrators. That is, to learn to read blue prints and draw three-dimensional assemblies of how airplane parts are assembled, so people who couldn't read blue prints or English could see how to put parts together. It was challenging, demanding, and again another approach to studying form was learned.

The next years were intense, as they were for most young persons. The war, separation, moving from place to place, seeing far more of life than ever before, working at various jobs available, and questioning the mores of my background were valuable. Independence was thrust on me and I learned to be a person on my own, as did many women at that time. The world of art was far removed. Having one's husband return safe after months of B-29 missions in the Pacific was paramount. I began to paint again and to teach. My first student was a young man suffering deep anguish over his war experience who was able to express his feelings on canvas. His first painting was accepted in a juried show as the impact was so intense.

173

The after-war pressure to return to "normalcy" pressured women to go back to old patterns of acceptable mores. I became a housewife, as well as a mother, and my dear husband took on the obligations of getting a proper job that would provide economic progress. Also, opportunity for applied art was available in the small city where we lived—designing, decorating, and displaying for a gift shop. Partnership in this business on a part-time basis gave me valuable experience in learning what it means to invest one's time, energy and money in keeping a business going. I also learned more about teaching. I found it most rewarding to help customers learn to discriminate qualities of things.

The opportunity to teach art in the local community college and work with the public school art consultant came almost by accident. This, too, was a big event in my life, as I found teaching more rewarding than my own work—at least within the constraints of being a wife and mother, as those roles were defined at that time. My family was of paramount importance, and I could teach, and help others grow in and through art experience, and still fulfill my family obligations.

To establish the program as an integral part of the college, I began a Master's degree at Central Washington College (now University). Reino Randall and Frank Bache, early Northwest art education film makers, were teaching there. Art education was mainly media centered with concern for teaching. But they gave me freedom to pursue my own ideas. I received my first introduction to psychology in an excellent overview course of the field in its many aspects in the 1950s. I became fascinated with what might be possible linkage between art and psychology. But for a Master's thesis I returned to an older interest and wrote a comparison of trends I saw in design processes and concepts of interrelations of physical interaction, as I could understand them, in the physics of that period. Somehow I felt that since humans are part of the universe, the ordering processes of universal things might be related to the cognitive ways we make order in our constructs and design of the environment.

The Stanford Years

1954-1957

At graduation my advisor bluntly told me I should go on for a doctorate. That if I did not do it then I never would. This challenge, to the horror of family and friends in 1954, set us in a new direction. My husband left business to finish his war-interrupted undergraduate education and was on his way to becoming an anthropologist, our son started first grade, and I was accepted into Stanford Graduate School.

Again, the interaction of social systems intervened. Ray Faulkner was very interested in the relationship of psychology to art, but he was then the Liberal Arts Dean and could not advise me. The other art education faculty member had other interests but would fill the social role as advisor. A professor of General Science, Alvarez-Tostado was most interested in my concern for the relationship of design to physics, but there was no academic discipline that would sponsor such a degree program. Though influenced some by default, but mainly by a growing interest, I pursued my degree in the College of Education, which led to the first phase of my Perception-Delineation theory. The basic program at that time included required work in educational psychology, the sociology and anthropology of education, philosophy, curriculum, statistics and research methodology. One specialized on the basis of this core work.

Though my interests were strong and motivation high, my background education in art had not provided the critical and qualifying skills I needed. After a year of course work, the single most important academic event happened. I flunked my comprehensive written exams. These 3-day exams were in the psycho-social foundations as well as art education which I did pass. This event caused a radical change in my approach to the work. Professors Pauline Snedden Sears, a psychologist who in actuality was my advisor, and George Spindler, an anthropologist, each let me write a paper a week for a quarter re-working my materials prepared for the exams. I learned to question, assess and evaluate sources and make careful, qualified assessments, and passed the repeat exam.

Then began a two year period as Instructor of the art education undergraduate courses and researching and writing my dissertation. Two events stood out at this time. I well remember the Saturday spent in my office where the theory took form after months of study. It was an experience as I have had many times as a painter; when through intuition, based on much preparation the factors of a whole go together.

I owe much to psychologist Pauline Sears, a Professor of Education whose challenges helped me get the dissertation written and defended. At the oral exam, a philosophy of education professor chaired and asked all the questions. He was determined his logic would uncover weaknesses in my defense, but my preparation was sufficient and [I]was passed with honors. Also, the day I graduated I had a call from a new publishing company asking me to write a book based on my dissertation. This began the three years of writing the first edition of *Preparation for Art* which went through three drafts. This book drew upon my materials from the psychology of perception, creativity, early studies of cognitive style and anthropology and the effect of culture on human behavior as they related to creating and learning through art.

Early Professional Work

1957-1962

After graduation, I started five years of teaching graduate art education at Stanford and formalized the doctorate program. Guy Hubbard and Mary Rouse, Ron Silverman, Arthur Efland, Warren Anderson, Gordon Kensler, Harold McWhinnie, and Dick Salome were among that diverse group. We explored relations between some of the aspects of the social and behavioral science as related to art, perception, cognitive style, child development, and creativity, as well as studying art and society.

My husband had begun his graduate studies in anthropology and I shared, with our son, the invaluable experience of some of his field work with the Blackfeet Indians. We owe so much to them because not only did we gain knowledge of their culture through their willingness to talk to us, but we also gained a much more profound respect for human dignity by witnessing theirs.

During this period I had a Ford Foundation grant through the College of Education in which we experimented with a curriculum of design problem-solving tasks for academically superior adolescents to see if we could increase creativity as measured by Guilford's pen and pencil creativity tests designed for people in the sciences. As had been reported, this study did show that our students did significantly improve their scores compared to a matched group of students who did not have the six-months course (McFee, 1968).

My previous experience was limited to West Coast art education. After *Preparation for Art* came out, I started lecturing nationally and conducting workshops and courses at other universities meeting art educators and seeing new programs in each place. Manuel Barkan, Julia Swartz, Reid Hastie, Ken Lansing, Vincent Lanier and Fred Logan were of particular interest to me. I also met two young men with exciting ideas on a panel at a Museum of Modern Art Education Conference in Chicago, David Ecker and Elliot Eisner. At the 1957 New York NAEA conference, I first met Ken Beittel and Mary Lou Kuhn. These four younger people seemed to me to be pushing the perimeters of what Art Education was to become. They had stimulating perspectives about 1) the philosophical assumptions underlying what we were doing, 2) curriculum development, 3) the actual behaviors of artists in drawing and curriculum development, and 4) the populations we could reach.

I also had the opportunity to meet a generation of people who had led the field before that. At that New York Conference, Victor Lowenfeld read my dissertation and encouraged me by noting we were in our infancy in understanding child art—and that my work would make a contribution.

I also met Mildred Fairchild with her world view of art education and was impressed over the years with her continued emphasis on making art education possible in the situation people were in. Edmund Ziegfeld was very active in establishing INSEA through the United Nations.

The Arizona Years

1962-1965

These were years of great contrasts. My husband had finished his degree and we were hired verbally by the University of Arizona, but my contract was never signed by the President because of nepotism laws. We were encouraged to come anyway by Deans who assured us it would be worked out, but it wasn't. I was unemployed. But this proved to be a precious, useful period. My young son was adjusting to a new place so I could spend much of the first year with his new found world of the desert and horses. The area out of Tucson with its lights and colors, its dry air, and the nature of people who lived in the desert, had a strong impact on us all. We built a desert house and I learned to ride again.

I was busy with visiting professorships and was free to accept more lecturing assignments. The opportunity to work with faculty and students in different regional cultures of our society was most educational. Florida State, Indiana, Western Reserve, Kansas State Universities, the Universities of Hawaii and Alaska, and in one state the University of Illinois, Northern Illinois, and Illinois State University illustrate some of the contrasts. The background experiences, the values, all contributed to my growing sense of the diversity within this country. Seeing the differences in student populations in institutions in Illinois, for example, helped me gain more awareness of the complexity of American society as sampled through college groups.

This provided an opportunity to see more of the cities I visited. Many cities were in turmoil then. I would try to find people who would take me to the most deprived and riot-torn areas. The images seemed so real when I was back home writing about art education experiences for children.

One assignment during that time was to lecture and participate in one of the early Canadian Art Education Conferences with Abram Maslow. On the final day of the conference, that great man and I shared the stage to reflect on our contributions to the meeting. I was reporting on my creativity research which I had tried to control as thoroughly as possible. A participant asked Dr. Maslow, "Why should art educators do research such as McFee's when they could soar with their ideas as you do?" He so graciously cautioned the young man who asked the question, that only after years of careful cautious work should one dare to soar. He also spent time with me encouraging me in my work and not to be afraid to take a stand as a woman.

Soon an opportunity opened up in Arizona to consult with the Phoenix school district helping teachers in South Phoenix work with the very diverse and often impoverished students there. My chapter in the NSSE yearbook described some of the things we learned as we studied those children (McFee, 1965). This was my first in-depth analysis of the conditions of poverty, racial and economic discrimination and its effects on school children in an urban setting. The challenge was to help art teachers become aware of the value differences between themselves and the children they were trying to teach. As teachers became more aware they reassessed their goals, made more effort to reach children where they were, and reported they enjoyed the teaching more.

Then I was hired to teach at Arizona State University and developed and processed through the various committees the doctoral program in art education. I did not stay long enough to see any of those students finish, but Susan Mayer, Virginia Brouch, and Ann Taylor were three outstanding students in my classes.

The Penn State Seminar in 1965 was a cornerstone in the development of art education (Mattil, 1966). During the ten-day conference, art educators presented parallel papers with psychologists, sociologist, artists, and philosophers. It most clearly identified the foundational fields of art education and opened up more connections as a basis of furthering research. It was during my most intense work with teachers of economically deprived students that I prepared my paper to be presented with the sociologist Melvin Tumin. The dialogue and interaction between all the participants and observers gave us a much broader definition of our field.

The Oregon Experience

1965-1981

In 1965 my husband and I were both offered positions at the University of Oregon where we have remained ever since. Art Education was a department in a school predominated by architecture and landscape architecture. The faculty I most identified with were in those departments. It was an extensive growing time as I was exposed to their ideas. Their dominant professional roles in those departments were not seen so much as aesthetic decision makers, but as catalysts in the social-physical design process, helping people make more qualified decisions about the built environment. My position was to develop an Institute for Community Arts Studies, for which the University had received a sizable grant, as well as teach in art education.

The Institute has had several major projects over the years—each of which was a learning experience. We worked with Oregon Communities to help them analyze how the form of their towns developed and the values and forces that were affecting it in the present. We involved study task groups of townspeople from all walks of life and teams of university students to study the environment and structural needs of different segments of the society. Art and social studies teachers and students in high schools participated in analyzing their uses of space in the community and report on it to town councils.

An environmental design curriculum was evolved with a countywide school district and teacher in-service workshops held. In all these activities, resources of the Department of Architecture, Urban Planning and Landscape Architecture were utilized as well as public school personnel. The interaction of our ideas with these groups was invaluable in developing our curriculum.

One of my agreements for coming to Oregon was that I could also start a doctoral program in art education. So these two activities went on side by side. Jessie Lovano came with me as the first doctoral student. If the five who are finishing dissertations complete this spring (1981), 45 doctorates in art education will have been granted in the years since 1965.

Also during the early years at Oregon I wrote the second edition of *Preparation for Art*. Jessie Lovano (later Lovano-Kerr) helped with library research. The work in environmental design I was doing also enlarged my horizons of what art education could include. At that time I was president of the Pacific Arts Association and arranged the Salt Lake City conference. As far as I know, it was the only conference totally focused on the art in the environment. The reviews of the conference were very positive but how far reaching or long lasting the impact I don't know. Fred Logan was one of our speakers and some of us hoped to carry on this work on in the national organization.

I had a grant from the American Institute of Architects Education Committee to write a book for children about cities. The committee was very diverse in their values. Some were socially aware, concerned, progressive architects. Others wanted a sophisticated book about "what was good about cities" for upper middle and upper class children. From my background of work in different economic and cultural situations, I wanted a book that was useful to all children in all kinds of situations. Art educators in different parts of the country helped me test it in low and middle income urban neighborhoods. The research is reported in *Studies in Art Education* (Fall, 1971) and I adopted the material for my last book *Art Culture and Environment* written with Rogena Degge (1980), adapted reprinting (1992).

Also, after going to Oregon I became co-editor and editor of *Studies in Art Education* with David Ecker and then with Manuel Barkan. The task of setting standards, editing, and sending manuscripts back two and sometimes three times for rewriting was challenging. Working with the different perspectives of the other editors was certainly an expanding process. We were carrying on a tradition of the founders and former editors, Beittel, Eisner, Hausman, and Lansing.

While on the board of the NAEA, an effort was made to stop publishing *Studies*. It wasn't stopped. Each of the editors, and many since, has had to defend its value to the NAEA Board. Each subsequent editor, Mary Rouse, Mary Lou Kuhn, Donald Jack Davis, and Laura Chapman, has brought new refinements to *Studies* and the last, Miami University's Sandra Packard, has been a most successful and disciplined editor, as she in turn passes the editorship to Ron MacGregor. Each of these editors has also had an effect on my experience as an art educator and certainly on the field. Two of them were my students and one a student of a student.[2]

The experience on the Board of the NAEA, convinced me that I could contribute more by writing and research than by being in a political position. So I have not accepted invitations for nomination for national office since.

The years at Oregon have been most rewarding, though there was resistance to the ideas of a doctoral program in the art and the art education departments, it is now well accepted. This program, as it now functions, is so much a part of my life that I must include it in this paper. Our students have high standing with faculty in the College of Education in the social and psychological foundations and in curriculum, in psychology with perceptionists, in anthropology, and in computer science.

One of the strongest influences on my ideas has come from working with graduate students at Stanford, briefly at Arizona State, and for the years at Oregon. Graduate students, much more directly than one's peers, force one to clarify the content of one's teaching and they provide direct feedback. These very diverse, very intelligent, experienced classroom teachers, from different cultures, backgrounds in art and teaching, have, in a sense, been my teachers. Most were students in small classes, in individual study, and I directed or was on most dissertation committees. While my subject matter mainly came from my own interdisciplinary research, the honing and focusing was strongly influenced by having to teach this material to doctoral students at Oregon: Robin Wasson and Diana Kendall from Australia, Graeme Chalmers and Ron MacGregor from Canada, Mahvash Arjomand from Iran, and from this country Jessie Lovano-Kerr, Rogena Degge, Beverly Jones, Linda Ettinger, Karen Hamblen, Mildred Roske, Ray Higgens, Joan Kurz Guilfoil, Barbara Boyer, Martin Rayala, Nancy Johnsen, Jean Ellen Jones, Mike Youngblood, Kristin Congdon, and Bill Thompson were very challenging. James Smith and Althea Williams taught me much about the dimensions of race and human dignity. But all the students contributed and I profited from working with each one of them. Many people speak of their own great teachers, but I think it is a two-way street, that whom you have the opportunity to teach is very important.

During these last 15 years, two sabbaticals and summers have provided opportunities to see the cultures of the Pacific and Europe. In the Pacific I actually saw the places I'd learned about in high school—Freemantle, the New Hebrides, Fiji, Honolulu, Prince Rupurt, Ketchikan, and Anchorage, with all the cultural and environmental differences they represent. There were two times to live a few months in both Sydney and Singapore, and then return to both cities seven years later. This provided the opportunity to photograph changes in two British colonial cities' public spaces as used by people with oriental and occidental cultures. The impact of comparing body languages, use of space, relations to others and design of public spaces has even more strongly affected my understanding of the impact of culture on cities. More clearly I see cities as collective, organismic art forms built out of the socio-cultural complex of values of the people who build and use them. This earlier study made, London, where we lived six months, and other great cities visited, seem so much more alive as their past merges into the present through the lives and cultural life styles of the people who mold and change them.

181

Implications from Professional Conferences and Institutes

1965-1981

One of the important developments in our field is the increase in interdisciplinary art education conferences that have had particular influence on my development and that I have been able to contribute to. Of course, the Penn State Seminar in 1965, as already mentioned, was a milestone for the field.

Through the years, the National conferences have included some aspects of interdisciplinary study, particularly in the Seminar for Research that Elliott Eisner, Ken Beittel, and I started. The Council on Policy Studies has addressed the nature of our field as an issue, but has become absorbed by pressing political issues in recent years. Different interest groups each draw on different foundational areas such as environmental design, special education, social aspects of art, and museum education. But it has mainly been other meetings that have appealed to more specific interests that have at the same time had broader interdisciplinary character.

I participated in the planning and carrying out of one of the Aspen Seminars, sponsored by CEMRL with Stan Madeja, focusing on psychology and art. The opportunity to interact with psychologists whose work I had used for some years was particularly stimulating.

One of the most serious research conferences I ever attended was the Women's Caucus meeting at Ohio State University in the spring of 1980. Most of the papers presented focused on critical problems in the actual education of children. Less socialization and more work transpired.

Being a keynote speaker at the INSEA World Conference in Australia was a highlight of my recent years. The focus was on the many dimensions of cross-cultural understanding through art. Most important was the contact with world leaders in art education, and with artists, philosophers, sociologists, and anthropologists who all contributed to this topic. One the personal rewards of that conference was to meet people who were still using *Preparation for Art* in South America and Europe, as well as in Arab countries and Japan, where it was published in those languages. After the conference I visited and lectured at twelve Australian teacher training institutions and helped plan the first Master's degree in Art Education. Contact with all those art educators and students was rewarding indeed. Art training there is much more thorough and demanding of students and education much more structured.

The most recent interdisciplinary conference was the National Symposium for Research in Art at the University of Illinois. In giving the conference overview, I had the opportunity to study the work of the major presenters; Howard Gardner, and Ellen Werner on child development in the use of artistic metaphors, Charles Osgood on the development of the semantic differential and recent work on a graphic differential, and Rudolph Arnheim's challenge of our emphasis in Western art on perceptual rather than conceptual realism. It was interesting to see their work in the context of broader interdisciplinary studies of child art from the last thirty years.

This points up one of the crucial research problems of this era. So much study has gone on in many different fields that relate to development and response in and to art that it behooves us all to tap findings that have not been replicated in each related area to see if we are taking the known findings into account. With computer retrieval centers becoming so much more accessible, it is easier to do. But it does require that our doctoral programs be more interdisciplinary so we can use the material we find across disciplines wisely. Also, our research methodology courses must include the use of retrieval systems. One wonders what other pertinent research lies buried in some library. One shocking experience was to find that in 1924 a comprehensive national study of child development in art had been done in 1923-24 and none of it had I discovered used in our literature. Psychologist J.B. Watson, as well as child development specialists, were used on the committee with supervisors. It supersedes all our development theory in art education and should be replicated today (McCarty, 1924).

To make this report more complete, I must record one other institution of vital importance to my works. The central and consistent study of Christian Science has influenced what I sought to understand of art and society, both of the individual and among world cultures and affairs. *The Christian Science Monitor*, with its world view of human dignity, progress and universal equality, has been a constant companion. I have always tried to keep church and state separate in my work as a teacher in public universities, but an acknowledgment of this religious influence on my work is appropriate here.

Implications for the Future

1981

Needs for the future of our field, as I see them at this point in my experience, are related to the changing social climate of our country. Certainly we will have to rely on our own resources far more than ever before, as teachers and as members of a professional field.

We will not be able to afford the luxury of quibbling about the different approaches and goals of art educators. We must open up the avenues of communication between us and utilize the strengths of each perspective. We must all be more concerned for the content of art, its history, modes of criticism and practice in a broad range of applications as they serve the individual and society.

Art is a major means of communication among people. We must teach it as such and see that it stays in every school. The impact on the quality of life, as communicated through the visual arts, is compounded by television and computer imagery. To understand, preserve and create visual quality as it relates to the rest of human life and many cultures requires the broadest educational base if we are not to live in the most dismal of worlds. It requires that our definition of visual quality allow for cultural diversity without succumbing to watered down mass conformity. The new technologies must be monitored and criticized in the same way, and we must not be afraid to use them constructively in education and in art so that their qualitative contributions can be strengthened.

Each of us as individuals need more skills in designing our personal and collective use of space so it is satisfying to us and contributes to the quality of the lives of others, as we all have less to work with and smaller spaces in which to do it. We must learn to design in process and not just seek static solutions. What gives me courage is the human capacity to innovate, design, to order, to refine, to render, recreate, and to critique. We have the capabilities to revitalize our cities and suburbs and preserve what is left of our natural environment ("and save some quiet, peaceful spaces for country folk as well").[3] Just a concern for visual quality and art won't do it. But a concern for art as it relates to the individual and to society can have an impact.

Notes

[1]Abstractions and adaptations from.
[2]Ronald MacGregor, Mary Rouse, and her student, Sandra Packard.
[3]Handwritten phrase on the original manuscript by my dear life companion.

References

Mattil, E. L. (1966). A seminar for research in art education for research and curriculum development. Office of Education, Dept. of H.E.W. Project No. V002, University Park: The Pennsylvania State University.

McCarthy, S. A. Ed. and chairman. (1924). *Children's drawings, a study of interests and abilities by The Child Study Committee of the International Kindergarten Union.* Baltimore: Williams and Wilhuis Co.

McFee, J. K. (1965). Art for the economically and socially deprived in 64th NSSE Yearbook, Reid Hastie, Ed.

McFee, J. K. (1968). *Creative problem solving of academically superior adolescents,* monograph, National Art Education Association.

McFee, J. K. (Fall 1971). Children and cities: an exploratory study of urban middle and low income neighborhood children's response to studying the city. *Studies in Art Education. 13*(1).

McFee, J. K. (1979). Society and identity: a personal perspective. In J. Loeb (Ed.), *Feminist college: Educating women in the visual arts.* New York: Teacher's College Press.

McFee, J. K., and Degge, R. M. (1977). *Art Culture and Environment.* Belmont, CA, Wadsworth. Paperback Kendall Hunt. Dubuque, IA, 1980. Adapted reprinting 1992. (Second edition in press.)

OTHER SELECTED BIBLIOGRAPHIES

BOOKS

McFee, J. K., & Degge, R., (1997). *Art, Culture, and Environment.* Belmont, CA: Wadsworth Publishing Company, Inc. Second Printing, Kendall/Hunt, 1980; adapted reprinting 1992.

Preparation for Art, (1961). Belmont, CA: Wadsworth Publishing Co. 8 printings: Japanese edition, 1967; second edition, June 1970.

CHAPTERS IN BOOKS, etc.

"A Study of 'Perception-Delineation': Its Implications for Art Education," *Research in Art Education*, 9th Yearbook of the NAEA, 1959, pp. 9-14.

"Art for the Economically and Socially Deprived," Chapter 7 in the *64th NSSE Yearbook*, Reid Hastie, Ed. 1965, pp. 153-175.

"Art Education for Talented Students," *The Encyclopedia of Education*, The Macmillan Company, 1971.

"Art and Society" in H. Feinstein, Ed., *Issues in Discipline-Based Art Education Seminar Proceedings*, Los Angeles: The Getty Center for Education in the Arts, 1988, pp. 24-25,104-112.

"Cultural Dimensions in the Teaching of Art," in F. H. Farley and R. W. Neperud, Eds. *The Foundations of Aesthetics, Art, and Art Education.* New York: Praeger 1988, pp. 225-272.

"Change and the Cultural Dimensions of Art Education" in *Context, Content and Community in Art Education: Beyond Post Modernism.* Ronald W. Neperud, Ed., New York: Teachers College Press. 1995.

ARTICLES AND REPORTS

"Children and Cities: An Exploratory Study of Urban, Middle, and Low Income Neighborhood Children's Response to Studying the City," *Studies in Art Education, 13*:1 (Fall, 1971), pp. 50-59.

"Art Ability" in *International Encyclopedia of Education*, Oxford: Pergamon Press, 1984.